Columbia University

Contributions to Education

Teachers College Series

No. 578

AMS PRESS
NEW YORK

A Study of Library Reading
In the Primary Grades

By
C. DeWitt BONEY, Ph.D.

TEACHERS COLLEGE, COLUMBIA UNIVERSITY

CONTRIBUTIONS TO EDUCATION,

No. 578

*Published with the Approval of
Professor* JEAN BETZNER, *Sponsor*

BUREAU OF PUBLICATIONS

Teachers College, Columbia University

NEW YORK CITY

1933

Library of Congress Cataloging in Publication Data

Boney, Cecil De Witt, 1902-
    A study of library reading in the primary grades.

    Reprint of the 1933 ed., issued in series: Teachers
College, Columbia University. Contributions to educa-
tion, no. 578.
    Originally presented as the author's thesis, Columbia.
    Bibliography: p.
    1. Reading (Primary). 2. Children's literature--
Study and teaching. I. Title. II. Series: Columbia
University. Teachers College. Contributions to educa-
tion, no. 578.
LB1573.B67 1972   372.4'14   76-176579
ISBN 0-404-55578-0

Reprinted by Special Arrangement with Teachers
College Press, New York, New York

From the edition of 1933, New York
First AMS edition published in 1972
Manufactured in the United States

AMS PRESS, INC.
NEW YORK, N. Y.   10003

ACKNOWLEDGMENTS

IT IS with pleasure that the author expresses his appreciation to Professors Annie E. Moore, Jean Betzner, and J. R. McGaughy for their generous assistance and encouragement during the process of this study.   He is indebted also to Professors Thomas Alexander and Arthur I. Gates for their helpful suggestions, and to the several hundred teachers who rendered invaluable services in collecting data.   To Myrtle Elizabeth Boney are due inestimable praises.

C. D. B.

CONTENTS

CHAPTER   PAGE

I. THE PROBLEM   1

II. THE DEVELOPMENT OF THE OBJECTIVES FOR LIBRARY READING
IN THE PRIMARY GRADES   4
The Colonial Period   4
The Period of American Authorship (1776–1840) . . .   6
The Period from 1840 to 1880   8
The Period from 1880 to 1916   11
The Present Period (1917 to 1932)   25

III. LIBRARY READING IN THEORY AND PRACTICE   31
Objectives for Conducting the Library Reading Program .   32
The Use of the Library Reading Materials   33
The Frequency of the Library Reading Period   34
The Length of the Library Reading Period   35
Work of the Teacher During the Library Reading Period .   35
Work of the Children During the Library Reading Period .   37
The Sharing of Reading Experiences   37
Relationship Between Library Reading Period and Story
Hour in the First Grade   41
Work of the Teacher and the Children During the Story
Hour   42
Checking upon the Books Read   44
Type of Reports Used for Sharing Reading Experiences   45
Books for the Library Reading Program   46
Selecting the Library Reading Materials   48
Source of Library Reading Materials   49
Preparation of Reading Materials   50
Teaching Children to Use and Care for Books   51
Means of Stimulating Interest in Reading   53
Home Reading.   53
Records   53
The Time of Year for Beginning the Library Reading Pro-
gram in the First Grade   55
The Furnishings Needed for the Library Reading Program   56

CONTENTS

CHAPTER   PAGE

IV. RECOMMENDATIONS AND CONCLUSIONS 58

    Function 58

    Time Devoted to the Library 58

    Work of the Teacher 59

    Work of the Children 59

    Materials 60

    Equipment 60

    Techniques 61

    Conclusions 62

BIBLIOGRAPHY 63

APPENDIX 67

CHAPTER I

THE PROBLEM

THE use of juvenile books has greatly increased during the past few years. The report from the White House Conference on Children's Readings shows clearly the recent demand for children's books and the efforts made by publishers to meet this need. The report states:

Since 1900 the market for children's books has grown enormously. At no time in the history of printing has there been such a wealth of suitable books as are produced constantly to supply book stores, and hence, homes and libraries. Since the war publishers have given more and more attention to their juvenile departments, often employing specialists with library experience to serve as advisers. In 1928, it was estimated that one-seventh of the total number of books published were juvenile. Whereas children's books were once considered an item almost exclusively for the Christmas book market, they now sell the year round as steadily as adults' books.[1]

Correspondingly, the emphasis which courses of study and professional reading books place upon extensive reading in the primary grades, and the full support given this movement by teachers since 1924, show that although still in its infancy extensive reading is growing rapidly.

Fourteen courses of study published between 1917 and 1923 give attention to library reading in the primary grades, whereas forty-seven courses published between 1924 and 1931 advocate this type of reading. Only three of twenty-nine professional books on reading published between 1915 and 1923 deal with library reading, whereas twenty-five of forty-six professional publications dealing with the teaching of reading published between 1924 and 1931 recommend this program to teachers. These facts would indicate that library reading is becoming an integral part of the primary reading program.

One study has been made of library or extensive reading to determine its value in building up reading skills in the second,

[1]*White House Conference on Child Health and Protection.* "Children's Reading," p. 14. The Century Company, 1932.

third, and fourth grades. This reading was "done in a classroom situation by the pupils in their regular classroom reading periods from material adapted to their reading ability and chosen by them individually under guidance of the teacher from many books."[2] This type of reading instruction was compared with that in classrooms where the children did their reading from several copies of the same book. The result of this experiment showed that both methods are equally effective in building up general reading ability in grades two, three, and four. The author of the study recommended that both extensive and class reading be used in the same classroom and ". . . that extensive reading be used more than class reading since it has more value for the development of desirable attitudes and habits in reading, in addition to equal effectiveness in building up general ability."[3]

The term library, or extensive reading, is used in a broader sense in this study than in the above study. It refers to the reading done by children in the classroom or outside the classroom; it does not include work based on series of readers which are commonly known as basal and supplementary readers, or teacher assignments in connection with some classroom course.

It is the purpose of this study to set forth the origin of the aims that have produced library reading, and to examine the techniques for conducting the library reading program as advocated by professional writings, courses of study, and classroom teachers. Such a study should answer or throw light upon some of the following questions: What is the purpose of library reading? How did that purpose originate? When should the books be used? Should there be a special period for reading? What is the work of the teacher and the children during the special period? What provisions should be made for sharing reading experiences? What are the values derived from a story hour? How often should there be a story hour? What is the relationship between the story hour and the library reading period? What is the work of the teacher and the children during the story hour? What kinds of reports should be given? Should children be required to report on the books read? What kind of reading materials should be used? Who should select these materials? What sources should be used

---

[2]Field, Helen, *Extensive Individual Reading versus Class Reading*, p. 3. Contributions to Education, No. 394. Teachers College, Columbia University, 1930.

[3]*Ibid.*, p. 49.

for securing materials? Should children be taught the care and the use of books in conjunction with the library reading program? What means are employed to interest children in books? Should children use the library reading materials at home? Should a record be made of the books read? Should first grade children use the library reading materials before they begin to read? What furniture is needed for the library reading program in the primary grades?

The historical facts needed to answer these questions were obtained from references found in the New York City Public Library, the Columbia University Library, and the Teachers College Library. Information on the library reading program as advocated by educators was obtained from professional writings published between 1924 and 1931. Information on the library reading program of schools was obtained from courses of study on file at the Bureau of Curriculum Research, Teachers College. Information concerning the library reading program used by teachers in the field was obtained by means of a questionnaire filled out by 254 teachers in various sections of the United States.

CHAPTER II

THE DEVELOPMENT OF THE OBJECTIVES FOR LIBRARY READING IN THE PRIMARY GRADES

LIBRARY reading is used in the primary grades as a means of attaining the objectives underlying present-day reading instruction. These objectives, like those in each period of our national development, determine the type and quantity of reading materials used. In the Colonial period the objectives were narrow—therefore a small amount of reading matter sufficed; in the present period they are broad—therefore many and varied types of books are used. In order to determine the origin of the aims that have produced library reading it is necessary to examine the aims prevailing during each period, and the types of materials used for reading instruction.

THE COLONIAL PERIOD

Reading played a small part in the lives of the early Colonists. The scarcity of books, the lack of interests outside the immediate locality, and the diversification of the home occupations to satisfy the necessities of life made oral expression the common means of communication.[1] But the religious convictions of these Colonists required that they read the Bible.[2] This furnished the impelling motive for most men to read and to see that their children received reading instruction. The schools of the times, wishing to satisfy this desire, used either parts of the Scriptures or other liturgical materials to teach reading.

Along with the Bible and the Psalter were used *The Horn Book*, *The New England Primer*, and various spellers. *The Horn Book* was the first book used in teaching reading in America.[3] It seems to have enjoyed great popularity throughout the Colonial period.

[1]Reisner, E. H., *Nationalism and Education Since 1789*, p. 335. The Macmillan Company, 1927.

[2]Andres, C. M., *Colonial Folkways*, p. 150. Yale University Press, 1919.

[3]Smith, Nila B., *An Historical Analysis of American Reading Instruction* (manuscript), pp. 22–52. Teachers College, Columbia University, 1931.

According to Miss Smith, "It was used in two capacities; for catechising in church and for giving children their reading instruction in school."[4] *The Horn Book* was supplanted by Benjamin Harris's *The New England Primer*, which was published about 1690. Ford gives us an idea of its popularity:

For one hundred years this Primer was the school book of the dissenters of America, and for another hundred years it was frequently reprinted. In the unfavorable locality (in a sectarian sense) of Philadelphia, the accounts of Benjamin Franklin and David Hall show that between 1749 and 1766, or a period of seventeen years, that firm sold thirty-seven thousand one hundred copies. . . . An over conservative claim for it is to estimate an annual average sale of twenty thousand copies during a period of one hundred and fifty years, or a total sale of three million copies.[5]

The content of *The New England Primer* was in accord with the purpose that it served. The first part contained the alphabet, consonants, double letters, capitals, and a syllabarium; these were the tools considered necessary so that a child could learn to read The Lord's Prayer and the Creed which followed. Ford says in describing the part which this book played:

In the apocryphal poem of John Rogers "unto his children" which was included in every New England Primer, he said:

> "I leave you here a little booke
> For you to look upon,
> That you may see your father's face
> When I am dead and gone."

No better description of the New England Primer itself could be penned. As one glances over what may truly be entitled The Little Bible of England, and reads its stern lessons, the Puritan mood is caught with absolute faithfulness.[6]

The motive for reading instruction at that time was of a religious nature and *The New England Primer* reflects this. Man was no longer to make intercessions to God through a church or a priest. As Ford says,[7] each soul was "morally responsible for its own salvation; and this tenet forced every man to think, to read, to reason." Ford continues:

. . . the children were taken in their earliest years and drilled and taught to believe what they were to think for themselves when the age of discretion was

[4] *Ibid.*, p. 27.
[5] Ford, Paul L., *The New England Primer*, p. 19. 1897.
[6] *Ibid.*, p. 1.
[7] *Ibid.*, p. 2.

reached.   And this was the function of The New England Primer.   With it millions were taught to read that they might read the Bible; . . .[8]

Miss Smith's study of Colonial readers shows that greater importance was attached to subject matter than to method.   She says:

It is quite obvious that the subject matter of early reading instruction was a much more important consideration than was the method of teaching it.   Method was considered incidentally as a tool in furthering the more fundamental aim of acquainting children with the materials needed in their early religious life and equipping them to read the Bible in meeting the needs of their later religious life.[9]

THE PERIOD OF AMERICAN AUTHORSHIP (1776-1840)

While *The New England Primer* continued in use more than one hundred and fifty years, its sales were on the decline at the beginning of the nineteenth century.[10]   The decrease in popularity of this old reading text was due to the publication of readers which expressed new ideas.   These, like the impelling force of religion in the former period, expressed the beliefs of the common people. Saving souls from perdition was no longer the central thought, but emerging into the social, political, and religious life of the day was the spirit of nationalism.   The new Republic used this emotion to bind together a provincial people who looked with suspicion upon all centralized power.   To inculcate nationalism in the minds of the young people it was thought wise to teach patriotism and good citizenship.   This was done through stories which extolled the country and gave examples of a good moral life.

The first book of this period really to affect the teaching of reading was Noah Webster's *An American Selection of Lessons in Reading and Spelling*, published in 1783.   This book was as decidedly patriotic as *The New England Primer* was moralistic.   The fifth edition which was published in 1790 contained orations and essays on the American Revolution.   Many of the straight informational pieces reflected the ire underlying the Revolution.   In relating some of the facts concerning the royal government of Georgia, the author says:

[8]*Ibid.*, p. 3.
[9]Smith, Nila B., *op. cit.*, p. 59 (ms.).
[10]*Ibid.*, p. 19.

It has just begun to recover from the low state to which it had been reduced by the narrow policy of the English government when the late war commenced.[11]

It would have been anomalous if it had not included some of the religious content. On the title page we find the statement that the book is calculated "to improve the minds and refine the taste of youth." This reader did not emphasize patriotism for long; in a later edition, published in 1809, less than one fourth of its pages were devoted to this new doctrine. In place of patriotic tales, stories which might be called historical or geographical were included, but by far the greater portion of the content was moralistic in nature.

Other school books which devoted some of their pages to patriotic subjects were the Lyman Cobb Readers. The most popular of these was *The North American Reader* published in 1835. Although these books appeared more than fifty years after the Revolutionary War they were decidedly nationalistic. Of the 416 pages in the *The North American Reader*, 122 were designed to instill patriotism; 28 of these contained the Declaration of Independence and government proclamations.

The moralistic imprint upon the readers of this period was far more indelible than patriotism. There was nothing new about this reading material which purported to teach morals, for such teaching had made its appearance in *The New England Primer* and *The Horn Book*. But in those books it had played a secondary part since their main purpose was to prepare for the future life. In this period it was one of the controlling motives that determined the content of books for reading instruction. Between 1776 and 1840 several readers were written with the definite intention of training in morals.

Notable among the readers which served the purpose of character education was Bingham's *The American Preceptor* published in 1795. Examination of this book shows that though it was written a few years after the close of the Revolutionary War it contained only five pieces which seemingly were chosen for the purpose of fostering patriotism. Some idea of the content of the book can be gained from the preface:

. . . the author has been strictly rigid in selecting such pieces only as shall have a direct tendency to lead the scholars in the path of virtue and religion, as well as to improve their taste in reading.

[11] Webster, Noah, *An American Selection of Lessons in Reading and Spelling*, p. 99.

The English Reader, which Lindley Murray published in 1822, emphasized elocution and morals. The following gives a very accurate description of its contents:

Pieces in prose and poetry selected from the best writers. Designed to assist young persons to read with propriety and effect; to improve their language and sentiments; and to inculcate some of the most important principles of piety and virtue.[12]

Other readers of this time which purported to instruct the child in the use of certain words and to entertain him with moral tales were *The Franklin Primer*, *The Improved Reader*, *The Classbook*, and *The Popular Reader*. These books are representative of the material published during this "Period of American Authorship" as it has been named by J. J. Mahoney[13] and R. R. Reeder.[14]

If the purpose of reading instruction, as expressed by the authors of these readers, is indicative of the pedagogical motive for teaching reading, the necessary reading material was bountifully supplied. For beginning reading, a book containing the alphabet, capitals, and a syllabarium was needed; *The New England Primer* supplied this want. To teach patriotism, a book denouncing England and eulogizing America was needed; the readers by Cobb and Webster met this demand. Stories for moral instruction were necessary; such tales occupied a prominent place in all readers, but an ample supply could be found in the Bingham and Murray readers and in *The New England Primer*.

THE PERIOD FROM 1840 TO 1880

It is a precarious undertaking to ascribe dates to historical movements which are the product of slow evolutionary growth, but if we think of the period from 1776 to 1840 as a time when readers were greatly affected by the spirit of nationalism and the aims of moral education, then the following period, which lasted until 1880, marked a renewal of reading materials with moral objectives increased, emphasis upon elocution, and the rise of the movement to adapt reading matter to the child. As a result of these objectives for reading instruction, graded series of books were published which were attractive not only because of their physical make-up, but also because of their interesting content. These features and

[12]*Op. cit.*, Title page.

[13]Mahoney, J. J., "Readers in the Good Old Days." *Educational Review*, pp. 217–226, October 1916.

[14]Reeder, R. R., *Historical Development of School Readers, and of Method in Teaching Reading.* The Macmillan Company, 1900.

the provisions for the repetition of vocabulary are indicative of an effort to apply two psychological laws of learning, readiness and exercise.

There are indications that the influence of Pestalozzi which spread in this country in the early part of the nineteenth century had much to do with bringing about these changes. According to this leader, the principles of education are inherent in human nature, and the materials of instruction are to be developed in such a manner that the physical, intellectual, and moral capacities of the child will be developed. One can readily imagine the influence which the application of these principles must have had upon the reading instruction of that day when one book was frequently used for several stages of reading, and very little effort was made to make the readers attractive to the child.

The first disciple of Pestalozzian educational theories in America was William McClure who, with Joseph Neef, a coadjutor of Pestalozzi, started in 1809 the first school in this country based on the new theories. Their first experiment was not successful. It remained for their later work at New Harmony, which was organized in 1826, to influence American education. Men who became protagonists of the Pestalozzian movement either because of the work of William McClure and Joseph Neef or because of their personal contact with the German schools where the new doctrine found fertile soil were William Russell, William C. Woodbridge, A. Bronson Alcott, Lowell Mason, Horace Mann, and Henry Barnard.[15] The writings of Horace Mann in his reports to the Massachusetts Board of Education did much to disseminate Pestalozzi's theories in this country. He was interested in reading, and his continuous attack upon the alphabet method of teaching beginners to read and his praise of the word method which he saw used in Germany doubtless had great effect upon the character of the new readers.

A few quotations from the *Common School Journal* which was edited by Horace Mann will show his interpretation of Pestalozzi's theories. He said:

I do not see, indeed, why a child should not learn to read as easily as he learns to talk by hearing the names of things, the utterance of which is accompanied by some action indicating to what things the respective names belong.[16]

[15]Monroe's *Cyclopedia of Education*, Vol. IV, pp. 657–59.

[16]Mann, Horace, "A Lecture on the Best Mode of Preparing and Using Spelling Books." *The Common School Journal*, Vol. 5, p. 25, January 1, 1842.

Concerning the word method of teaching reading he said:

> But it seems to me by far the most legitimate and efficient way of introducing a
> child to the knowledge of our language is through the meaning of the word used.
> The avenue is always open, and is always pleasant; it is established by nature and
> exists in the constitution of the human mind.[17]

He made a criticism of existing readers which no doubt was responsible for many of the improvements made in the new readers.

> Most of our primers as I have mentioned are adapted exclusively to the method
> of teaching by spelling, or to that of teaching by the whole word at once, and are
> therefore not well suited to a language like ours, which, by its construction, demands
> the use of both methods—one, of those classes of words which are regular,—the
> other, for those which are irregular, in spelling and pronunciation.[18]

Concerning content Horace Mann said:

> But most of our school books fail, I think, in their arrangement, and in the se-
> lections of pieces quite above the comprehension of the readers.   They should be
> more simple, more conversational, and more like everyday business and matter of
> fact life.[19]

The importance which he attached to building upon the child's interests becomes clear from the next two quotations:

> To sustain the interest of the child in the subject matter of his studies, whatever
> that may be, is of primary importance.   Such an interest is indispensable to prog-
> ress.[20]

He continued:

> If we would know how to please children we must know the source of the pleasures
> which children derive from a perception and knowledge of objects.[20]

As a result of these objectives, many sets of readers were published between 1840 and 1880, some of which attained national distribution.   Among the most popular were the six-book series by William McGuffey; the six-book series by C. W. Sanders and J. C. Sanders; the six-book series by G. S. Hillard; the National Series of Readers by Richard G. Parker and J. Madison Watson; and the Progressive Series by Salem Town and Nelson M. Holbrook.

The emphasis upon elocution in these readers is evident in their

[17]*Ibid.*, p. 28.
[18]*The Common School Journal*, March 15, 1844, p. 315.
[19]*Ibid.*, December 2, 1844, p. 364.
[20]*Ibid.*, Vol. IV, p. 26, January 1, 1842.

content and in prefatory statements.   The first sixty-three pages of *Hillard's Sixth Reader* are devoted to a treatise on elocution by Professor Mark Bailey, instructor in elocution at Yale College. Seventy-three pages of the *Fifth Reader* of the National Series by Richard G. Parker and J. Madison Wilson are devoted to elocution. And the *Manual of Reading in Four Parts: Orthophony* by H. L. D. Potter, a professional book for teachers published in 1871, devoted its 418 pages to class methods, gestures, and elocution. Following are a few statements taken from the prefaces of several readers that show the attention given to elocution: From *The National Third Reader* by Parker and Watson, 1866:

> It has been our purpose in preparation of this volume to furnish the facilities necessary for the cultivation and improvement of the voice, and the acquisition of skill in reading and delivery.

From *Hillard's Fourth Reader* by G. S. Hillard and L. J. Campbell, 1863:

> It contains a great variety of words and sentences for training the voice and forming a distinct articulation.

The following statement from *The Progressive Third Reader* by Salem Town and Nelson M. Holbrook, 1857, while showing the emphasis on elocution, indicates that an effort was made to arouse the interest of the child.

> One of the objects aimed at in the selection of the reading lessons has been to present such a variety of subjects and styles of composition as will render the book interesting and instructive, and at the same time furnish exercises well adapted to discipline the vocal organs and secure a natural and easy manner of reading.

After reading these statements one is impressed by the fact that great importance was attached to elocution, while little or no attention was given to reading attitudes. There were two reasons for this emphasis upon oral reading: first, it was a means of assuring the teacher of the child's vocabulary knowledge and, second, oral reading played an important part in the common life of the day.

THE PERIOD FROM 1880 TO 1916

As in the previous period, the changes made in reading instruction between 1880 and 1916 were the result of new objectives.

Pestalozzi's theories which had been instrumental in producing graded readers took on a more tangible aspect when the educators of this time demanded that instruction develop in the child a love for reading and teach him to appreciate good literature. These motives first expressed themselves in supplementary readers which were used in both the primary and the grammer grades. Soon it was discovered by upper grade teachers who were attempting to attain the new goals that sets of readers did not suffice. The common complaint against them was that they were too narrow in content; they were not adequate for the experiences in literature which were thought necessary. To meet the demand for a more enriching reading program there were placed in the upper grades a variety of books which marked the beginning of upper grade classroom libraries. These libraries enjoyed a phenomenal growth from their beginning in the latter part of the nineteenth century. As a result of this success and because of two later movements of this period—emphasis upon silent reading and the child experience curriculum—library reading was started in the primary grades of the schools.

Development of the Objectives

Teaching reading in order to develop a love for it and to cultivate a taste for good literature were aims expressed at this time as a reaction to the emphasis upon phonics, elocution, and the confinement of reading to the narrow scope of the basal readers. The campaign for the establishment of these new reading objectives was carried on by many practical school men and educators. The most frequent charge against the old method was that too much attention was given to the mechanics of reading at the expense of training the child in what to read.

J. H. Smart, Superintendent of Public Instruction of Indiana, in the *Twenty-Eighth Report of the Superintendent of Public Instruction*, demanded that teachers develop in children a love for reading. He stated:

It is not enough that our instructors teach children to read. They must cultivate in the children a taste for that which is wholesome. They must introduce their pupils to the best authors. It is not enough that the teacher point to the library. . . . The teacher must go with the pupil to the library and show him what to get, and how to use it after he gets it. . . . I quote from a lecture recently delivered before the teachers of Quincy by Charles Francis Adams, Jr.

"It is the fault of a system which brings a community up in the idea that a poor knowledge of the rudiments of reading, writing and arithmetic constitutes in itself an education. Now, on the contrary it seems to me that the true object of all your labors as real teachers, if, indeed, you are such . . . the great end of the common school system is something more than to teach children to read; it should, if it is to accomplish its full missions, also impart to them a love of reading."[21]

A popular book of this time, and one of the first professional books for teachers, was *The Sentence Method of Teaching Reading, Writing and Spelling*, by George L. Farnham.[22] In this book the author gave breadth to the motives for the teaching of reading by advocating that the child be induced to read what he desires to know.

Commenting upon the aims of reading instruction, Dr. G. Stanley Hall said that proper instruction should give "a living appreciation of good literature, and a habit of reading it, rather than bad, for with this end all others are secure."[23]

The Committee on Relations of Public Libraries to the Public School reported to the Council of the National Education Association in 1899 that it was not the main purpose of reading instruction to teach the child what to read or how to read, but that it was the conviction of leading educators that the reading program should develop an appreciation of worthwhile literature. Dr. Charles A. McMurry, a member of this committee, stated:

To teach children how to read so that they could make use of books, newspapers, etc., was once looked upon as a chief object of school work. We now go far beyond this and ask that teachers lead the children in the field of choice reading matter and cultivate in them such taste and appreciation of a considerable number of the best books ever written that all their lives will be enriched by what they read. . . . It is not a question of learning what to read—all children who go to school learn that; it is a vastly greater question of appreciating and enjoying the best things worth reading. . . . So profound has been the conviction of leading educators upon the value of the reading matter of the schools for the best purposes of true education that the whole plan of study and the whole method of treatment and discussion, as touching these materials, have been reorganized with a view to putting all children into possession of this great birthright.

To prove this we will state briefly a few of the changes which have already taken place in many of our best schools:

[21]Smart, J. H., "Books and Reading for the Young." *Twenty-Eighth Report of the Superintendent of Public Instruction of Indiana*, p. 98. Pub. by Carlon and Hollenbeck, Indianapolis, Ind., 1880.

[22]Farnham, George L., *The Sentence Method of Teaching Reading, Writing and Spelling*, pp. 49–50. C. W. Barden, Syracuse, N. Y., 1881.

[23]Hall, G. Stanley, *How to Teach Reading and What to Read in School*, p. 24. D. C. Heath and Company, 1886.

1. Good literature of high quality, from the fertile brains of the greatest writers, has been put into every grade of the common school from the first year on.

2. In the first three grades, since children have not yet learned how to read, but are in the process of acquiring this art, they must get their introduction to the best stories suited to their age by oral presentation of the teacher.[24]

One might ask how the practitioner felt toward this new movement. Dr. W. T. Harris, Superintendent of Schools at St. Louis, dealt with the purpose of reading instruction in an address on "Textbooks and Their Use," which he gave before the National Education Association in 1880. He stated as his belief that "the child should be taught how to read, but this is not enough; he should be taught how to understand and verify what he reads. Nor is this enough; he should be taught what to read. . . ."[25]

According to Nila B. Smith, the new emphasis in reading was due to some extent to the Herbartian movement which stressed the importance of children becoming acquainted with good literature. She says:

In tracing the cause of the new emphasis it would have been very much more convenient if one had found that it began in 1890 instead of 1880, because then it would have been quite obvious that it was a direct product of the move of Herbartianism which swept the country in the nineties, due to American educators who returned from study in Germany and who published reports between 1889 and 1897. As a matter of fact, there is abundant evidence that the new emphasis in reading instruction was well under way in the eighties. Even so, it seems more than likely that the movement was a reflection of the Herbartian principles which were so active in Germany at that time and which undoubtedly affected American practice before our prominent Herbartian protagonists lent their efforts to bringing the movement to a climax in American schools.[26]

The Development of Supplementary Readers

As one can readily surmise, any effort to comply with the new aims for reading would have demanded either a radical change in the one tool for teaching reading, the basal reader, or the introduction of new reading material. The latter method was followed, and sets of supplementary readers were published. While it was still believed that a basal reader was necessary to teach the elements of reading, it was thought that supplementary readers would satisfy the new aims of reading in all grades, and in addition

[24] "Report of the Committee on Relations of the Public Library to the Public School." *Proceedings of National Education Association*, 1899, p. 473.

[25] Harris, W. T., "Textbooks and Their Use." *Proceedings of National Education Association*, Vol. 19. 1880, p. 105.

[26] Smith, Nila B., *op. cit.*, p. 178 (ms.).

to meeting these demands would strengthen the vocabulary learned in the phonics lessons.

A statement from the Textbook Committee of the Boston Public Schools in 1881 shows that school people expected to develop the child's sense of values in regard to literature by means of the supplementary readers:

Your committee are of the opinion that the value of supplementary reading as a means of cultivating taste for good reading has not been overestimated and the results have proved that the action of reading books was a wise and judicious one and the use of such books should be encouraged and continued.[27]

A statement from the Board of Supervisors of the same city supports the purpose of supplementary readers as stated by the Committee on Textbooks and also shows how they were to be used:

The books supplied for supplementary reading are intended to be used for two distinct purposes:

1. For oral reading in the classroom, that pupils may learn to communicate to others readily and well the thought of an author. That reading should be chiefly reading at sight.

2. For silent reading in school and at home, that pupils may gather information or cultivate a taste for good literature or both. After a hundred or more words are thoroughly learned from the blackboard, the pupils need a rich supply of easy, carefully graded supplementary reading to develop and fix in the memory the vocabulary of first and second readers.[28]

Statements from the prefaces of two books published at that time indicate that supplementary readers were to satisfy a need for good literature and a demand for variety of reading matter.

The demand for variety of reading matter adapted for use in primary grades has called forth the book.[29]

This volume is presented to the public in the hope that it may place directly in the hands of pupils the supplementary literature needed.[30]

Many supplementary readers were published to meet the growing demand. Among the earliest of these were the *Standard Supple-*

[27]Committee on Textbooks, *Supplementary Reading.* School Document No. 14. Boston Public Schools, 1881.

[28]Board of Supervisors, *Supplementary Reading.* School Document No. 7. Boston Public Schools, 1881.

[29]Rickoff, Rebecca D., *A Supplementary First Reader.* (Preface). 1892.

[30]Pearsons Eleanor A. *Our Country in Poem and Prose.* (Title page). 1899.

mentary Readers by William Swinton and George R. Cathcart published in 1880 by the American Book Company, and the *Harper's Educational Series* published by the same company in 1880 and edited by O. T. Bright and James Baldwin. Another supplementary book which came into use a little later was *Our Country in Poem and Prose* by Eleanor A. Pearsons, published in 1899. In courses of study published between 1905 and 1920 much emphasis was placed upon supplementary reading. An examination of 229 courses of study for primary grades issued throughout the country between 1889 and 1919 showed that 80 gave some attention to supplementary reading. But mechanics were still the order of the day, for 138 of these school manuals were highly concerned with the intricacies of reading.

The content of the supplementary readers was similar to that of the basal reader, the distinguishing characteristic being that they were thought to be easier than the latter. Usually each teacher had several sets of books available for use throughout the school year. The lesson was conducted in the same way as a lesson from a basal text, the main difference being that the reading was more extensive.

The growth of the use of the supplementary books in the teaching of reading is indicated by F. M. Crunden, Public School Librarian, St. Louis:

> We have now two hundred and sixty-nine sets of books for circulation in the schools. Each set consists of thirty copies of books carefully chosen for a certain grade. It is better to send thirty copies of the same book than thirty different books. . . .
> These sets of thirty are sent to the schools on request of their respective principals to be kept two weeks with the privilege of renewal two weeks more. The books may be used in any way the teacher prefers—either in school or at home.
> Various kinds of books are chosen according to the interest of the child.[31]

Mr. Crunden submitted the following question to the teachers who had been working with supplementary reading materials: "What value do you attach to literature and supplementary reading in connection with the school curriculum?" He quoted ten teachers and principals who spoke most highly of the use of such material.[32]

---

[31]Crunden, F. M., "The School and the Library—Value of Literature in Early Education." *Proceedings of National Education Association*, 1901.

[32]*Ibid.*

Even though "teaching children to love to read" and "to have an appreciation of good literature" were aims which were glibly quoted at this time, practitioners who had accustomed themselves to teaching reading mechanics could not change their methods instantaneously; they used these readers to strengthen the vocabulary which had been learned in the phonics lessons. The following statement is indicative of this use:

> Learning to read through the science of phonetics gives the child such a mastery over new words that it is difficult to find enough material properly graded from a phonetic point of view to satisfy his increased power. The "Beacon Introductory Second Reader" has been carefully compiled to meet this want.[33]

The use of supplementary readers as a means of vocabulary drill was declared necessary by Robert C. Metcalf in a report on supplementary reading made to the National Education Association in 1899. He states:

> Experience has seemed to prove that the art of reading must be carefully taught during the first six years in the school and success in teaching depends largely upon the abundance of practice, which requires an abundance of time.[34]

Upper Grade Classroom Libraries

Supplementary readers did not continue to satisfy, if ever they did, teachers in the upper grades as a means of developing a taste for good literature. These books had been used primarily for vocabulary drill and had served as additional books for oral reading. As a result very little actual change was achieved by this new program. But immediately afterwards or almost simultaneously with the development of supplementary readers there grew the movement to have many kinds of books brought into the classroom to augment the study of history, science, and geography, and to provide a wide literary reading program for the children. This use of books marked the beginning of the upper grade classroom library which was a potent factor in starting a similar program in the primary grades.

Statements from educators who advocated a large variety of books in the classroom are interesting not only because they express

---

[33]Fassett, Jane H., *A Beacon Introductory Second Reader.* (Preface) 1916.

[34]Metcalf, Robert C., "Supplementary Reading." *Proceedings of National Education Association,* 1899, p. 470.

the belief that such a program offers a means to a desired end, but also because they are indicative of a certain conception of primary reading.   According to them, there could be no appreciation of literature until the child learned to read fluently.   The only incentive for the young child to learn to read was future opportunity for using this tool.   For this reason, the early classroom libraries did not affect the reading in the lower grades where supplementary readers were in continuous use for a number of years.

The cause for classroom libraries was presented by S. Louise Arnold in her book *Reading: How to Teach It*, published in 1899. In writing on supplementary reading Miss Arnold implied that this type of work was no longer of value to upper grade students, for their reading was done with a purpose, but that it served its most important function in the lower grades where training was given in ability to read.   She wrote:

> Of course this provision becomes useless as soon as the pupils have passed the "learning to read" stage, and are reading for the sake of thought getting only, without reference to training in power to read.   Then the supplementary reading should be chosen purely with an eye to throwing light on other subjects studied, or for their literary value, and pleasure in reading.   Mention has been made of the value of school libraries as an aid to the reading habit.   Here the Supplementary Reader loses its title, and advances to the grade of a "real book."   Now the cultivation of the reading habit and the love of books is an immediate aim, and the book ceases to serve as a test merely.   It is a means to an end, an instrument by whose use new knowledge can be gained or the pleasure of life enhanced.   Therefore, it is wise to spend carefully the money devoted to books, buying few of a kind, and many kinds now.   For reference, for individual reading, for reading to the class, this collection of books is invaluable.   The skillful teacher will plan many exercises which will reach far beyond the immediate lesson in their beneficient results.[35]

Gradually the formal reading program became less important. The following statement is indicative of a feeling that children who have mastered the mechanics should read from a wide range of easy books:

> After the second year, when all pupils should be fluent readers of anything they can understand there need be no distinction made between supplementary reading and regular reading.[36]

Prior to this time Dr. G. Stanley Hall had advocated the enrich-

[35]Arnold, S. Louise, *Reading: How to Teach It*, pp. 206-07.   Silver, Burdett and Company, 1899.

[36]Spaulding and Bryce, *Learning to Read; A Manual for Aldine Readers*, p. 71.   Newson and Company, 1907.

ment of the various subjects by means of reference books. He said:

> A single text gives a narrow individual view of a subject at the best. In geography, e.g., a dozen or two books on the country studied are shown the pupils in school and circulated among them. They are perhaps stimulated to·read a chapter of travels here, or a section on natural history or physical geography there, and report it in school. . . . Thus pupils learn to handle books, how to taste and smell them, how to skip, to take time to select, and that half of education consists in learning where and how to get information.[37]

The report of the Committee on Relations of Public Libraries to the Public School did much to hasten the progress of the upper grade classroom libraries. In this report Robert C. Metcalf interpreted "supplementary reading" to mean all books except textbooks and such reference books as dictionaries and encyclopedias,[38] while Dr. Charles A. McMurry stated that it was the duty of the teacher to guide the child toward good literature, such, for example, as *Hiawatha*, *Pilgrim's Progress*, and *Gulliver's Travels*.[39]

The development of classroom libraries was due in a large measure to both public and school libraries which emphasized the importance of acquainting children with an abundance of books. A. W. Cole, librarian of Jersey City Free Library, in an article in the *Library Journal* for April, 1895, indicted the public school for not teaching the child what to read, and to further his argument he quoted from George E. Hardy who said:

> The great problem of the day is not to teach our children how to read, but what to read.
> If we fail to do this and content ourselves with giving the child the mechanical ability to read, we are leaving him in possession of a power that is equally potent for evil as it is for good.

In an address before the Library Department of the National Education Association in 1903 C. B. Gilbert showed there was unanimity of opinion among librarians and educators concerning the value and use of an ample supply of books. In addition he placed upon the teacher the duty of familiarizing the child with the

---

[37]Hall, G. Stanley, *How to Teach Reading and What to Read in School*, p. 38. 1886.

[38]"Report of the Committee on Relation of Public Libraries to the Public School." *Proceedings of National Education Association*, 1899, pp. 466–72.

[39]*Ibid.*, p. 473.

library, and offered a plan for a constant source of books for the classroom library. He said:

> Granting then that the library should not in any way transgress the recognized and established work of the school, what can it do to supplement that work? That is, what should the children get from the public library?
>
> 1. They should get an acquaintance with an abundance of good books. Such books should be easily accessible, carefully selected but not too minutely selec.ed.
>
> 2. The children should get from the public library through this abundant supply of accessible books, a love for books.
>
> 3. They should get familiarity with the library itself.
>
> How are these desirable things to be accomplished? There are two methods advocated. One which I believe may fairly be called the "Buffalo Method,"— that of taking books from the library to the schools and supplying the needs of the children there, making the teachers assistant librarians.
>
> The other plan is that of supplying the schools with library cards which are distributed to the children, the teacher acting as a friend and adviser in the selection of books.

Soon after the introduction of classroom libraries it became evident that the outcome depended upon the resourcefulness of the teacher. She was responsible for providing the classroom with the needed books, and for guiding the child in the proper use of them. This thought was expressed in an article concerning library reading in the schools of the boroughs of Manhattan and the Bronx which appeared in *The Outlook* for December 2, 1899.

> The purpose of introducing the class library was to put the supplementary reading of the pupils more immediately under the guidance and control of the class teacher. This provides the class teacher opportunity to study the taste of the child who selects books for reading out of school and apart from school work; to bring the pupils and the class teacher into close relations outside of the routine work of the classroom.

The Growth of Upper Grade Classroom Libraries

No specific date can be fixed for the beginning of library reading. We have, however, two accounts of its early use in New York City. The first record of classroom libraries is given in the *Cyclopedia of Education*, edited by Paul Monroe in 1913, in which the statement is made that the work of supplying the classroom with books was begun in New York City in 1893. We cannot rely entirely upon this for *The Outlook* for December 2, 1899, contained this statement regarding the New York system: "The first classroom libraries were opened in September, 1897."

Classroom libraries grew rapidly. *The Outlook* of December 2, 1899, furnishes the following figures:

Last year 2,742 class libraries were established in the boroughs of Manhattan and the Bronx, containing 87,660 books which had a circulation of 872,370 during a single term.

The *Cyclopedia of Education* shows the increase in classroom libraries in twelve years:

There were in 1911 more than 12,000 classroom Libraries in the city (New York) containing from thirty to forty books each and with a circulation of 8,000,000 volumes a year.

A further record from the *Cyclopedia of Education* shows the development of classroom libraries in the principal cities of the United States in 1913:

Today practically all of the public library systems in the cities of the United States have organized school departments through which classroom libraries are placed in the schools. In Buffalo, the public library has placed 828 libraries in the grammar schools of the city from which 418,752 volumes were circulated in 1910. In St. Louis traveling libraries are sent to the grade schools. In 1911, 176 traveling libraries containing in all 101,759 volumes were sent to schools and deposit stations are established in ten school buildings in which 59,238 volumes are placed. The Cleveland Public Library appointed a supervisor of classroom libraries in 1906, and the use of classroom libraries is being developed as rapidly as the resources of the library will permit. Detroit sends books for supplementary reading to the schools, circulating 77,869 volumes to school children in 1910. In Pittsburgh a catalogue of books for the use of pupils for the first eight grades was published in 1902 by a committee of teachers and librarians. A second, revised edition was published in 1907. Books are sent to 108 schools; about 100,000 volumes are circulated for home use yearly, and nearly twice that number used in the classrooms. The Newark Public Library has a school department, maintains a reference room containing books and periodicals for the use of teachers, and sends about 500 traveling libraries to classrooms.

Primary Classroom Library Reading

About twenty years after the beginning of library reading in the upper grades, library reading in the primary grades became a part of the program for children who did not read fluently. Supplementary reading attained nearest to perfection in the primary grades and the proper employment of these books as well as the growth of the upper grade classroom libraries was no doubt an influential force in the development of the primary library reading program. In addition there were two other movements at that time which probably fostered the use of books in the first three grades.

The first movement was supported by a small minority who believed that reading should grow out of the child's interests and experience. This group was opposed to the practice of teaching the young child nothing but reading and writing.[40] Dewey, a member of this group, upheld this position by maintaining that the sensory organs and nervous system of the young child were not sufficiently developed. Professor Patrick discussed the question in the *Popular Science Monthly* of January, 1899, under the title "Should Children under Ten Learn to Read and Write?" His conclusions were that the emphasis given to reading in the first few grades was purely customary, and that it could not be justified. Huey predicted that the new curriculum would gradually develop in the children a desire to read. He stated:

> Whatever the elementary school course is to be, when worked out for our times, it seems certain that reading and writing are not to be taught for their own sake in the earlier years; that the work of the new curriculum will gradually develop a natural desire to read and to read for meaning; that it will give own experiences which will furnish the material for natural interpretation of suitable subject matter. . . .[41]

The conflict between oral and silent reading which produced the second movement held the attention of practitioners and educators for a decade and a half (1905–1920). The necessity of determining which type of reading should occupy the first place in the elementary grades was recognized at the beginning of this period when new reading materials were used as a pretext for additional oral reading lessons. The forces for more silent reading and less oral reading were not only numerically strong but the arguments they presented were backed by scientific evidence. In 1913 Rudolf Pintner conducted an experiment with twenty-three fourth grade pupils in which silent reading proved to be 40 per cent more efficient in the point of speed than oral reading.[42] E. E. Oberholtzer in 1914 tested 1800 children in grades three to eight for rate of silent and oral reading. The results showed superior averages for silent reading in all the grades.[43] In 1916 Judd reported a study of 1831 pupils from which he concluded that good readers usually read fast and poor readers read slowly.[44] In

[40]Huey, E. B., *The Psychology and Pedagogy of Reading*, p. 305. The Macmillan Company, 1908.

[41]*Ibid.*, p. 310.

[42]Pintner, Rudolf, "Oral and Silent Reading of Fourth Grade Pupils." *Journal of Educational Psychology*, Vol. 4, pp. 333–37, June, 1913.

[43]Oberholtzer, E. E., "Testing the Efficiency of Reading in the Grades." *Elementary School Journal*, Vol. 13, pp. 313–22, February, 1915.

[44]Judd, Charles H., *Measuring the Work of the Public Schools*. The Survey Committee of the Cleveand Foundation, Cleveland, Ohio, 1916.

1917 W. A. Schmidt showed the superiority of silent reading over oral reading by means of photographic records of the eye.[45]

The Development of Primary Classroom Library Reading

Various phases of library reading developed at different times and in different school systems. In 1897 it was discovered that some children in the third grade had a sufficient vocabulary for library reading, and the circulation of story books, including fairy tales, fables and attractive nature stories, among these children for school and home use was advocated.[46] This idea gained prominence between 1905 and 1915, during which time courses of study of many school systems stated that home reading books for primary grade children had been provided.[47] Some of these courses of study gave lists of home readings for the first grade.[48] A period for teachers and children to read library books was developed about 1907[49] and appeared in a course of study in 1910.[50] But it was not until 1911 that schools allowed children to use these library books at their leisure time.[51]

C. B. Gilbert, in an address before the Library Department of the National Education Association in 1903, stated that library books should be carefully selected and easily accessible.[52] But places where teachers might keep their library books were not suggested until 1911.[53]

It can readily be seen that many phases of our present-day primary library reading existed in the early days of the twentieth century though they were not incorporated in any one program. They occupied no definite place in the courses of study and seem to have been tacked on with a bit of uncertainty concerning their

[45]Schmidt, William A., *An Experimental Study in the Psychology of Reading*, p. 79. University of Chicago Press, 1917.

[46]Kaltenback, M., "Room Libraries." *Proceedings of National Education Association*, 1897, pp. 1021–1025.

[47]*Courses of Study and Annual Report of Eureka Schools*, Eureka, Calif., 1913, p. 21. *Manual and Course of Study*, San Bernardino County, Calif., 1909, p. 17. *School Manual*, Santa Clara County, Calif., 1911, p. 7. *School Manual*, Tulare County, Calif., 1911, p. 7. *Manual for Public Schools*, Tehma County, Calif., 1909, pp. 22–23.

[48]*Course of Study*, Orange County, Calif., pp. 22–24. *Manual and Course of Study*, San Bernardino, Calif., 1914, p. 16.

[49]*Course of Study*, Jackson Public Schools, Jackson, Mich., 1907, p. 5.

[50]*State Manual and Course of Study*, State Department of Education, Montgomery, Ala., 1910, p. 52.

[51]*School Manual*, Santa Clara County, Calif., 1911, p. 7.

[52]Gilbert, C. B., In *Proceedings of National Education Association*, 1903, p. 950.

[53]*School Manual*, Tulare County, Calif., 1911, p. 60.

value. It is difficult to say how much they contributed to the development of library reading in the primary grades, yet their existence indicates that they were the result of some realization of the child's love for extensive reading. Mechanics of reading were in the foreground and were emphasized in nearly all courses of study, professional books on reading, and educational periodicals, while very little was said about extensive reading. This over-emphasis on the mechanics of reading was, no doubt, a great handicap to the development of library reading.

The first recorded use of library books, or books which were not parts of sets of readers, in the teaching of beginning reading was made by Professor Annie E. Moore with kindergarten children in 1915. The purpose of this experiment, as stated by Professor Moore in the *Teachers College Record* of September, 1916, was to determine how children's initiative can be utilized in beginning reading. Books were placed in the classrooms along with other reading materials. With these books was "a large assortment of beautiful, separate illustrated rhymes and stories with accompanying titles that gave pleasure in a similar way." The materials and activities employed were of a kind which strongly appealed to children. The books were accessible to them throughout the day and were placed where they could be chosen from among other materials. Professor Moore stated that these children did not learn to read, which of course did not affect the result of this experiment since it did not attempt to teach them to read. She said:

They turned eagerly to books without the slightest pressure from the teachers and showed great persistence in mastering the difficulties encountered.

Speaking for the experiment, she said:

There is no doubt whatever in the minds of those who conducted and observed the experiment that the keen interest which was aroused by the charming pictures and the unusually fine social opportunity offered, gave a vivid impression of the printed word.

This experiment differed from previous studies in these respects: (1) It provided a rich environment of books and other interesting materials for primary grade pupils. (2) The children were allowed free use of these books, pictures, and other classroom equipment. (3) These books, pictures, etc., furnished an indispensable part of the program. Following this experiment other school systems began to include such a reading program in their courses of study.

In 1917 the *Manual of the Elementary Course of Study for the Common Schools of Wisconsin* departed from the traditional methods prescribed by courses of study and advocated a reading program very much in keeping with Professor Moore's experiment; but it adhered too closely to the reading mechanics, and library reading seems to have been added as an afterthought and regarded with some suspicion. The manual recommended a variety of books for the library and the use of low tables and chairs. To induce the children to read and look at books the teachers were encouraged to introduce books to the class by telling or reading aloud part of the story. Children were allowed to do library reading after they had finished their seat work.

The *Richmond Course of Study in English*, published in 1917, gave some space to this type of reading. It contains the following statement:

> Classroom libraries are formed almost entirely through the effort of the teacher and the coöperation which she secures from the children and the principal. In each classroom there should be a table or a shelf which contains books that children may read during seat periods and after the assigned work has been well done. Children waste much time in school because they are not profitably employed. To be accustomed to read during the spare moments is a splendid habit.[54]

It remained for the *Seattle Course of Study* of 1921 to give a broader scope to library or extensive reading. Heretofore primary reading had occurred only in the classroom and during the recitation period, but now the child was encouraged to read many easy books at home. Parents were provided with book lists for purchasing children's books. Time was set aside in the classroom program that the children might select books of interest and share their reading experiences. The *Seattle Course of Study* suggested that the teachers encourage the children to keep a record of what they read as a means of stimulating interest.

THE PRESENT PERIOD (1917 TO 1932)

Today, library reading is recognized in many professional reading books, courses of study, and classrooms as a definite part of the primary reading program. Much use is made of it as a

[54] *Course of Study in English*, Richmond Public Schools, Richmond, Va., 1918, p. 4.

means of realizing two of the present-day aims of reading instruction. These aims were expressed by the Reading Committee of the National Society for the Study of Education in 1925. They are: to "develop strong motives for and permanent interest in reading" and to "develop rich and varied experience in reading." The thought expressed in each aim shows clearly the influence of the aims of the preceding period. The first aim is a restatement of the aim of developing in the children a love of reading, while the second gives breadth to the idea of acquainting them with good literature. The new aims are due primarily to psychological, philosophical, and educational ideas based upon empirical studies.

Research of the last period and the beginning of the present period brought out many facts regarding children's interests and the rôle of reading in modern life which influenced the reading program. After the publication of the studies by Rudolf Pintner, E. E. Oberholtzer, William A. Schmidt, Charles H. Judd, and others which showed the superiority of silent reading over oral reading, and the experiment by Professor Annie E. Moore in 1915 which showed that children could profitably browse among many new books, additional impetus was given the movement for wider reading experiences by E. L. Thorndike, who not only questioned the formal reading program but ventured this conjecture:

Perhaps it is in their outside reading of stories and in their study of geography, history and the like that many school children really learn to read.[55]

In 1918 John Franklin Bobbitt broadened the reading program by stating in his book *The Curriculum* that "the way to make reading easy and rapid and pleasant is to have much reading from the first grade onward and an ever-increasing quantity from grade to grade. A selection that is so difficult as greatly to impede progress thereby proves that it belongs on a later level, and is to be prepared for by reading that grade upward to its degree of difficulty."[56]

By 1921 silent reading was established as a type of reading to be used primarily by elementary school children, and many professional books were published to aid the teaching of it.[57] At the

[55]Thorndike, E. L., "Reading as Reasoning: A Study of Mistakes in Paragraph Reading." *Journal of Educational Psychology*, Vol. 8, p. 332, June, 1917.

[56]Bobbitt, John Franklin, *The Curriculum*, Chap. XVIII. Houghton Mifflin Company, 1918.

[57]O'Brien, J. A., *Silent Reading*, Macmillan Company, 1921. *The Twentieth Yearbook of the Society for the Study of Education*, Part II, Silent Reading, Public School Publishing Company, 1921. Watkins, Emma, *How to Teach Silent Reading to Beginners*, J. B. Lippincott & Company, 1922.

same time W. W. Theisen, a member of the Silent Reading Committee of the National Society for the Study of Education, declared that "learn to read by reading" had become a familiar maxim. He cited evidence from the St. Louis Survey which showed that the best readers read extensively. He said:

> The general trend of teachers' opinions seems to be that good readers are produced by a large amount of reading. This contention is not without merit. Schools in which a large number of books is read in primary grades as a rule produce strong readers, in comparison with those where little is read; e.g. city vs. rural schools. In the St. Louis Survey a large proportion of the pupils were found to be reading many books silently during the second and third grades. In some classes the children read as many as one book a week. The tests showed that these children were markedly superior to those who did not have such opportunity.[58]

In evaluating an extensive reading program Theisen further said:

> The extensive reader acquires a wide field of experience, secures much practice in silent reading for thought, the thread of the story, or the points of interest. He becomes practiced in phrasing. His vocabulary is increased through acquisition of words whose meaning is gathered from the context.[59]

Evidently anticipating the future aims of reading instruction to "develop strong motive for, and permanent interest in reading," he attacked the common practice of teaching too much mechanics and ignoring the young child's interests:

> Of those [reading programs] purporting to be interesting, many are based upon shallow, superficial interests. In their earnest desire to have beginning children master a particular phonic system, teachers are in grave danger of overlooking the factor of interest. Most teachers probably do not make sufficient attempt to discover likes and dislikes of each child, and to build accordingly.[60]

Gradually the breakdown of the aim of teaching reading—an appreciation of good literature—became evident. Not only did it prove futile for this age, but as shown in Dr. Hosic's study, the methods which were used to attain this aim were usually deterrent to the appreciation of good books.[61] In his book *Modern Elementary School Practices* George E. Freeland advocated that

[58] *The Twentieth Yearbook of the National Society for the Study of Education*, Part II, Silent Reading, p. 16. Public School Publishing Company, 1921.

[59] *Ibid.*, p. 16.

[60] *Ibid.*, pp. 20–21.

[61] *The Twenty-Fourth Yearbook of the National Society for the Study of Education*, Part I, Reading, p. 121. Public School Publishing Company, 1925.

children be allowed to rise gradually to high levels of literature. According to this writer the young child is attracted by inferior literature, but under proper guidance and when exposed to interesting books of a higher order he will pass this stage.[62]

Between 1917 and 1925 the group advocating extensive reading gained adherents, because it was discovered that children disliked much of that which they were forced to read, and when they were permitted to select their own reading matter the results furnished clear evidence of a broad reading interest. As this knowledge confirmed a belief that wide experience was the best type of education, it was easy for the reading committee to conclude that one of the major aims of teaching was to "give rich and varied experience through reading."

Below are listed a few of the experiments made at the beginning of this century to discover the child's reading interest.

In 1921 A. M. Jordan obtained information from 3598 pupils nine to eight years of age concerning the books and magazines which they liked. The conclusions drawn from this study show the differences in the interests of boys and girls and the tastes of each group at various age levels.[63]   In the same year W. L. Uhl made a critical and constructive study of the content of school readers. The results of this study showed that these books contained much that was unsatisfactory.[64]   In 1922 Uhl asked eighty-two seventh and eighth grade pupils to report their reactions to a series of selections. This study brought out the fact that children are keenly interested in informational materials if they are well written.[65]   Dr. Fannie W. Dunn read forty paired selections to one hundred ninety-five different primary classes to determine the characteristics which account for increased interest. On the basis of this investigation it was concluded that surprise and plot appeal to both sexes alike, that boys are interested in stories about animals, while girls prefer stories about children and familiar experiences and to a lesser degree those containing repetition and

[62]Freeland, George E., *Modern Elementary School Practice*, pp. 131–32.   The Macmillan Company, 1921.

[63]Jordan, A. M., *Children's Interests in Reading*, pp. 43–91.   Contributions to Education, No. 107. Teachers College, Columbia University, 1921.

[64]Uhl, W. L., *Scientific Determination of the Content of the Elementary School Course in Reading*, p. 152. Studies in the Social Sciences, No. 4.   University of Wisconsin, 1921.

[65]Uhl, W. L., "The Interests of Junior High School Pupils in Informational Reading Selections." *Elementary School Journal*, Vol. XXII, pp. 352–60, January, 1922.

conversation.[66]   Another experiment of this time, conducted by Florence E. Bamberger, was influential in determining the effect of the physical make-up of books on children's selections.   Information with regard to the relative attractiveness of the physical features of a book was obtained by allowing children to make selections from several copies of the same book.[67]

Some significant facts furnished by modern life were another factor in the establishment of broad reading as one of the new aims. Intensive investigations to discover reading proclivities showed that intelligent reading is indispensable to active participation in modern life; they showed that the amount of reading done in our present-day life is increasing rapidly and that this amount varies greatly in the different sections of the country.[68]

Many studies were made concerning the function of reading in modern life and their results added momentum to the change in the reading program.   Rhey Boyd Parsons made a study of the reading habits of 314 adults distributed among eight occupational groups, while W. S. Gray secured conferences with more than 900 adults to discover what they read.[69]   C. H. Judd's quantitative study of newspapers and magazines showed that the number of these publications increased from 1880 to 1910 more than 500 per cent, while the increase in the population during that time was less than 100 per cent.[70]   Later a study of the reading in each state was conducted by Ward G. Reeder.   In 1922 he made the following statement concerning the country as a whole:

According to Ayer's American Newspaper Annual Directory for 1922, there were circulated in the United States each day last year 31,810,672 copies of daily newspapers, an average of more than one for each family.   Besides these daily newspapers there were distributed millions of copies of weekly newspapers, magazines and books.   The twenty largest magazines of the country had a combined circulation of 21,430,615, while the several thousand smaller magazines had a combined circulation of almost as large.[71]

[66]Dunn, Fannie W., *Interest Factors in Primary Reading Material.*   Contributions to Education, No. 113.   Teachers College, Columbia University, 1921.

[67]Bamberger, Florence E., *The Effect of the Physical Make-Up of a Book upon the Children's Selections.*   Johns Hopkins Press, 1922.

[68]Gray, W. S., *Summary of Investigations Relating to Reading,* p. 15.   Supplementary Educational Monographs, No. 28.   University of Chicago, June, 1925.

[69]*Ibid.,* pp. 9–15.

[70]Judd, C. H., "Relation of School Expansion to Reading." *Elementary School Journal,* Vol. XXIII, pp. 253–66, December, 1922.

[71]Reeder, Ward G., "Which States Read the Most?" *School and Society,* Vol. XVIII, pp. 235–40, August 25, 1923.

Thus in the beginning of this period of reading development the emphasis on silent reading, the importance attached to the reading interests of children, and the information on the broad reading interests of some adults made it inevitable that the aims stated for the teaching of reading would be broad.   In 1922 C. R. Stone gave the essence of the new educational thought in one of the aims which he developed for primary reading.   He stated that the purpose of primary reading is "to provide an extensive vicarious reading experience for all pupils, with provision for individual differences in ability and tastes."[72]   In 1923 H. Grove Wheat stated "that suitable reading material for pupils of the first grade is extensive rather than intensive and that it is to be derived from a variety of sources."[73]   In 1924 Mary E. Pennell and Alice M. Cusack claimed that the proper reading instruction "gave the child the ability to live a richer, fuller and more complete life."[74]   It remained for the Reading Committee of the National Society for the Study of Education in 1924 to express more fully the implications of the research and thought of the preceding fifteen years.   They are: "To develop rich and varied experience through reading; to develop strong motives for, and permanent interests in, reading."[75]

[72]Stone, C. R., *Silent and Oral Reading*, p. 38.   Houghton Mifflin Company, 1922.

[73]Wheat, H. Grove, *The Teaching of Reading*, p. 216.   Ginn and Company, 1923.

[74]Pennell, Mary E., and Cusack, Alice M., *How to Teach Reading*, p. 6.   Houghton Mifflin Company, 1924.

[75]*The Twenty-Fourth Yearbook of the National Society for the Study of Education*, Part I.   The Report of the National Committee on Reading, pp. 9–11.   Public School Publishing Company, 1926.

CHAPTER III

LIBRARY READING IN THEORY AND PRACTICE

IT IS the purpose of this chapter to examine (1) the objectives for library reading, and (2) the techniques for conducting the library reading program as advocated by professional publications, courses of study, and teachers who are using the library reading program in the classroom.

The data for professional literature were secured from twenty-five publications. They were selected by a close examination of fifty-six professional publications dealing with general methods of teaching reading and published since 1924. (See Bibliography).

The information from courses of study was obtained from forty-seven school manuals published since 1924. These were selected after a careful examination of 233 reading courses of study, general courses of study, language courses of study, and social science courses of study from city schools (public and private), county schools, and state schools throughout the United States.

The bases for selecting courses of study and professional publications were, first, that they deal with some phase of library reading, and, second, that they be written by well-known writers since 1924. This date was selected as a means of separating the present-day material from the historical, since the significant phases of the latter were treated in the previous chapter.

The data for teachers were secured by means of a questionnaire. Letters were written to primary grade teachers and supervisors soliciting their help in getting the questionnaire answered. Those who did not use the library reading program were asked to establish contact with teachers who did and who might be willing to coöperate in this study. This preparation made it possible to submit the questionnaire to persons interested, and as a result about 90 per cent of the questionnaires sent were filled out and returned. All of them contained usable data.

Answers were received from 94 first grade, 82 second grade, and 78 third grade teachers, a total of 254 teachers. They represent public and private schools situated in rural and urban communities in twenty-nine states.   Eighteen teachers are in platoon schools and the rest are members of organizations where one teacher teaches all the subjects in a classroom.   Twenty-five are teaching two or more grades.   A copy of the questionnaire appears on pages 67 to 70.

A copy of the questionnaire appears on pages 67 to 70.

OBJECTIVES FOR CONDUCTING THE LIBRARY READING PROGRAM

Objectives for the library reading program in the primary grades are stated by 44 courses of study, 18 professional publications, and 254 teachers, which is a high proportion of each of the sources of information.   These data are evidence that those who use this program and those who advocate it recognize its values.

Some of the data concerning the various phases of the library reading program have been put in tables for comparison of the support from each of the three sources.   In order that this comparison might be made easily percentages are used.   These percentages are not based upon the total number of courses of study, professional publications, and questionnaires from teachers used in this study, but in each table they are based upon the number that express an opinion on the topic considered.   Thus, in this way an attempt is made to discover the trends for conducting each phase of the library reading program from opinions that have been expressed.

The data in Table I show high agreement among courses of study, professional writings, and teachers with respect to the two objectives "Develop strong motives for and permanent interest in reading," and "Develop rich and varied experience through reading" for the library program.   This use of the two objectives stated by the Reading Committee of the National Society for the Study of Education indicates that both theory and practice have been influenced by it.   The remaining thirteen motives are specific, and in all probability they represent means for the realization of broader objectives.   There is, however, very little agreement on them.   A high percentage of the teachers check half of them, but very little support is given by courses of study and professional publications.   The implication is that the library reading program which stimulates the child to read of his own volition in and outside the classroom should be used as a means of attaining broad reading objectives.

TABLE I

PERCENTAGES OF 44 COURSES OF STUDY, 18 PROFESSIONAL PUBLICATIONS, AND
254 TEACHERS SUBSCRIBING TO OBJECTIVES FOR THE
LIBRARY READING PROGRAM

MOTIVES	PERCENTAGES		
	Courses of Study	Professional Publications	Teachers
Develop strong motives for and permanent interest through reading..............	77.2	94.4	86.6
Develop rich and varied experience through reading............................	45.4	44.4	82.9
Furnish more reading materials for children.	2.3	5.5	68.9
Furnish a means of using leisure time.......	4.6		49.9
Furnish a means of sharing worth-while reading experiences.......................		11.0	63.3
Create a desire to own books.............	2.3	5.5	
Develop care in the use of books..........	2.3		52.4
Develop an appreciation and love of good literature............................	20.5		
Develop a habit of keeping a list of books to read..............................		5.5	
Come to have favorite authors and know their characters......................		5.5	
Develop regular rhythmic eye movements...		5.5	
Develop ability to read and interpret at sight		5.5	
Aid in the room activity.................			43.1
Enlarge the child's vocabulary............			67.3
Aid the teacher in checking up on outside reading.............................			16.6

THE USE OF THE LIBRARY READING MATERIALS

The necessity of a special period and some free time for using the library reading materials is emphasized by more than the majority of the courses of study, professional publications, and teachers giving information on this topic (Table II).

Since most of these writings and opinions of teachers would have the children's interests broadened at each stage of their reading development, these provisions may be expected to produce results. While the materials are being used the teacher must have an opportunity for direct contact with the pupils, but time must also be provided when the children can turn to the reading materials of their own volition. The remaining provisions for reading show that each of the three groups from which information is drawn is revising the school program in an effort to find time for more library reading.

TABLE II

PERCENTAGES OF 24 COURSES OF STUDY, 18 PROFESSIONAL PUBLICATIONS, AND
254 TEACHERS MAKING PROVISIONS FOR USING THE LIBRARY
READING MATERIALS

PROVISION FOR USING LIBRARY MATERIALS	PERCENTAGES		
	Courses of Study	Professional Publications	Teachers
Special period..........................	54.2	77.7	56.7
Leisure time............................	50.0	55.5	74.0
Before and after school..................	17.6	11.1	
During the regular reading recitation.......	8.3		
All times throughout the day.............			34.4
When assigned work has been completed by the class.............................			16.9
During the seat work period..............		11.1	
During the regular reading period for those students in the first grade who are mature readers...............................		11.1	

THE FREQUENCY OF THE LIBRARY READING PERIOD

Little help is given by courses of study and professional publications on the frequency of the library reading period. Table III shows that no distinction is made by courses of study on the fre-

TABLE III

PERCENTAGES OF 7 COURSES OF STUDY, 7 PROFESSIONAL PUBLICATIONS, AND
131 TEACHERS REPORTING ON FREQUENCIES OF LIBRARY READING PERIOD

FREQUENCY	PERCENTAGES		
	Courses of Study	Professional Publications	Teachers
Daily in the first grade....................	28.6	71.4	52.5
Daily in the second grade................	28.6	85.7	31.7
Daily in the third grade..................	28.6	71.4	28.3
Twice a week in the first grade............	14.3		13.6
Twice a week in the second grade..........	14.3		26.8
Twice a week in the third grade...........	14.3		15.2
Once a week in the first grade.............	57.2	14.3	25.0
Once a week in the second grade..........	57.2	28.6	31.7
Once a week in the third grade...........	57.2	28.6	45.7

quency of this period in the three grades, and that very little is made by professional publications. These publications in scheduling this period have failed to recognize a difference in the mental development of the children in the primary grades and in their growth in reading ability.

The teachers, however, are very responsive, more than half reporting on the frequency of this period. It is to be noted that there is a gradual change in the frequency of this period from daily usage in the first grade to twice a week in the second grade and once a week in the third grade. This indicates that teachers are sensitive to child development. The very young reader needs more teacher guidance in handling books, in selecting picture books, and in getting the meaning of pictures than do third grade children who are familiar enough with the use of books and the technique of reading to require only one supervised period per week.

In addition, this departure from what is advocated by courses of study and professional publications shows that teachers are not bound by school manuals nor afraid to mold their own program to meet changing needs though unauthorized by professional publications.

THE LENGTH OF THE LIBRARY READING PERIOD

Teachers were not asked to give the length of their library reading periods; and courses of study did not include suggestions as to a desired length. However, some help on this question was found in three professional publications, a perusal of which disclosed this trend: the library reading period should be from five to ten minutes in the first grade and should gradually extend in length as the children grow in reading ability until it approximates twenty to thirty minutes in the third grade. It would seem that these recommendations are in accord with the nature of the child's span of attention.

WORK OF THE TEACHER DURING THE LIBRARY READING PERIOD

One would expect that the value of the library reading period would be determined in a large measure by the aids that are given children with their reading handicaps. But this conclusion does not seem to be held by many who advocate such a period, for only

7 courses of study, 9 professional publications, and 131 teachers make recommendations concerning the work of the teacher during the library reading period. Table IV shows the various duties assigned to teachers during the library reading period.

TABLE IV

PERCENTAGES OF 7 COURSES OF STUDY, 9 PROFESSIONAL PUBLICATIONS, AND 131 TEACHERS REPORTING VARIOUS TYPES OF WORK OF THE TEACHER DURING LIBRARY READING PERIOD

Teacher's Work	Percentages		
	Courses of Study	Professional Publications	Teachers
Give any assistance that will aid in the enjoyment of the reading....................	28.6		90.0
Give special assistance to slow and weak pupils..............................	28.6	44.4	34.3
Make note of children who are using materials not suited to them, who are restless, and who have bad training habits; give appropriate training during another period.....	28.6	33.3	2.8
Work with small groups..................	28.6	33.3	
Share reading experiences with individual and small groups......................	14.3	66.6	
Stimulate interest in reading materials by comments, by reading selections and encouragement	28.6	33.3	
Aid children in preparing stories to share with others.............................	14.3	33.3	
Have individuals report their reading experiences to the teacher................		11.1	3.0
Correct children's posture, manner of holding book, finger pointing, lip movement, etc...			30.0
Teach another class to report their reading experiences...........................			20.8
Check upon the library books for another week...............................	14.3		
See that a good atmosphere pervades.......	28.6		

The trend expressed is that the teacher should devote time to making this reading experience as enjoyable as possible. She must give much time to the slow and backward pupils so that they too may gain pleasurable experiences from the books. And while she should be aware of the reading defects she should not risk dampening the spirit of the period by doing remedial work, but should be content to make notes of defects for correction during another period.

Further evidence that a spirit of enjoyment should predominate this period is shown in Table IV by lack of support given to such practices as correcting bad habits and checking upon books.

WORK OF THE CHILDREN DURING THE LIBRARY
READING PERIOD

Two courses of study and seven professional publications express the belief that children not only should have adequate experiences with books, but they should also develop the work habits shown in Table V. There is indicated an effort to place upon the children responsibility for the conduct of the period. The value of this objective cannot be denied. The very nature of the program which trains children at a special period to use books during their leisure time requires that certain habits be fostered.

TABLE V

PERCENTAGES OF 2 COURSES OF STUDY AND 7 PROFESSIONAL PUBLICATIONS
ADVISING TYPES OF WORK OF CHILDREN DURING THE
LIBRARY READING PERIOD

CHILDREN'S WORK	PERCENTAGES	
	Courses of Study	Professional Publications
Children should realize that as far as possible the same atmosphere of quiet that prevails in the public library should be maintained here........................		57.2
Children should work quietly with the library reading materials without the immediate supervision of the teachers...	50.0	57.2
Children should formulate with the teacher standards for using the library reading materials.................		14.3
Children should read in low voices to the teacher.......	50.0	

THE SHARING OF READING EXPERIENCES

Approximately 88 per cent of the professional publications, 33 per cent of the courses of study, and 91 per cent of the teachers advocating library reading would have children share their reading experiences. Some of these state values to be derived from this experience in the classroom (Table VI).

It is noticeable that a high percentage of the courses of study and the professional publications included in Table VI use the sharing of reading experiences as a means of furthering interest in reading.

This objective was not included in the questionnaire; had it been, it is believed that a high percentage of teachers would have checked it. In addition, it is a means of enlightening the teacher as to the success of the child's thought-getting, thus eliminating the checking period. It also provides for an audience situation which calls for good oral reading. The three motives "develop discriminating tastes," "furnish an opportunity for introducing new books," and "aid in class coöperation" are supported by only one source of information. It is believed, however, that these are not only feasible but worthy objectives.

TABLE VI

PERCENTAGES OF 7 COURSES OF STUDY, 5 PROFESSIONAL PUBLICATIONS, 212
TEACHERS STATING OBJECTIVES FOR THE SHARING OF
READING EXPERIENCES

	PERCENTAGES		
MOTIVES	Courses of Study	Professional Publications	Teachers
Stimulate interest in reading..............	100.0	80.0	
Provide a means of checking reading experiences...........................	14.3	60.0	50.4
Furnish an opportunity for oral expression..		20.0	78.4
Provide an audience situation.............		40.0	66.7
Develop discriminating tastes.............		20.0	
Furnish an opportunity for introducing new books..............................			55.8
Aid in class coöperation..................			53.4
Furnish an opportunity for checking grammatical errors.........................			19.0

It is natural that courses of study, professional publications, and teachers should use any available time for the story hour since it is a relatively new demand upon the primary schedule.

A third of the professional publications and approximately a fourth of the courses of study have suggested that the story hour be at the language period (see Table VII). Small percentages from each of the three sources have suggested that the children share reading experiences before and after regularly established periods. There is very little demand that the sharing of reading experiences be done at the library reading period, which shows an endeavor to have this period free from any pressure which might keep individual children from enjoying their books.

The majority of each of the three sources recommend that the

TABLE VII

PERCENTAGES OF 13 COURSES OF STUDY, 9 PROFESSIONAL PUBLICATIONS, AND
234 TEACHERS MAKING SUGGESTIONS ON PROVISIONS FOR
SHARING OF READING EXPERIENCES

PROVISION FOR SHARING	PERCENTAGES		
	Courses of Study	Professional Publications	Teachers
During a special period or story hour.........	53.6	55.5	70.5
During the library reading period..........	07.7		06.8
During the opening exercise..............	07.7		01.7
During the language period..............	23.1	33.3	02.6
Use any available time..................		11.1	
At the close of and during a regular reading period.............................		11.1	
Time provided whenever children wish to share their reading experiences..........	23.1	11.1	
At the close of a day...................	07.7		
At such a time a story meets the day's needs	07.7		
Before a class recitation.................	07.7		
No time for reports.....................			12.0

story hour come at a regularly established period. This is evidence that this period is too important to be an appendage, but should become a definite part of the schedule. This period is variously termed "The Circle Hour," "The Conference Period," "The Book Club," or "The Story Hour," the latter being the most common name given it.

The data in Table VIII show that only five courses of study and five professional publications make suggestions on the frequency of the story hour. The recommendations are similar to those made with respect to the frequency of the library reading period. No recognition is made of differences in the mental ability and the reading ability of the children within the three primary grades. Thus these writings advise teachers to have the story hour occur as many times per week in the first grade as in the third grade.

According to Table VIII the story hour occurs in most cases once a week, as reported by 38.2, 49.1, and 61.1 per cent of the first, second, and third grade teachers respectively. If this percentage is compared with the rate for the first, second, and third grades having a daily story hour, which is 32.3, 10.5, and 1.8 per cent respectively, it will be seen that the weekly period increases gradually from the first to the third grade, while the daily period decreases. It will be recalled that the same is true of the library reading period. From this we may infer that the library reading period and the story hour, the period for reading and the period

TABLE VIII

PERCENTAGES OF 5 COURSES OF STUDY, 5 PROFESSIONAL PUBLICATIONS, AND
165 TEACHERS MAKING SUGGESTIONS CONCERNING THE
FREQUENCY OF THE STORY HOUR

FREQUENCY	PERCENTAGES		
	Courses of Study	Professional Publications	Teachers
Daily in the first grade....................		40.0	32.3
Daily in the second grade.................		40.0	10.5
Daily in the third grade...................		40.0	01.8
Twice a week in the first grade............			07.3
Twice a week in the second grade.........			10.5
Twice a week in the third grade...........	20.0		12.7
Once a week in the first grade............	60.0		38.2
Once a week in the second grade..........	60.0		49.1
Once a week in the third grade...........	60.0		61.1
Occasionally in the first grade............	20.0	60.0	10.3
Occasionally in the second grade..........	20.0	60.0	07.0
Occasionally in the third grade...........	20.0	60.0	07.4

for sharing, are logically connected with each other. The frequencies of both periods are inversely proportional to the child's reading ability and interest. In the third grade the average child is usually a fluent reader and is able to do much reading alone which he does not care to share with others; for this reason third grade teachers deem it advisable to have a weekly hour. The average first grade child is often handicapped by lack of vocabulary or interest. He needs not only considerable help from the teacher, but also the impelling motive of being able to share what he has read with others; therefore the daily story hour is almost imperative in this grade. Several first grade teachers state that the number of "story hours" per week is reduced in the latter part of the school year when the children begin to acquire the tools of reading. Children are then able to do independent reading, and the time is given over to the reading of library books.

Another indication of the gradual change from a daily story hour to one occurring at greater intervals is the fact that second grade teachers provide the highest ratio among those who state that the period occurs three times a week. Two teachers reported that they had the story hour as often as the children wanted it, and one teacher stated that she had the story hour when enough reports were ready.

RELATIONSHIP BETWEEN LIBRARY READING PERIOD AND STORY HOUR IN THE FIRST GRADE

According to four writers of professional reading books, method books, and teachers' manuals, the reading and the sharing of stories (the library reading period and the story hour) in the first grade are accomplished in one period. Charles J. Anderson and Isobel Davidson[1] state that little children desire to tell or read a part of their story to the teacher or to other members of the class soon after they have read it, and they are therefore allowed and often encouraged to share their experiences during this period.

The close relationship between the reading and the telling of a story in the first grade is particularly evident in Lois Coffey Mossman's description of a "Story Hour" of a "Library Club." She says:

When children enter the first grade they have no ability in reading, but they have a genuine love for stories and a delight in picture books. Utilizing these two interests of the children, a first grade teacher has been known to have an occasional period on the program given to the story hour club. It consists of two parts. The first is a silent period in which each child looks at a book which he selects from the library table. The book consists largely of pictures, beneath which are rhymes, couplets, or simple legends. The themes of these books are child favorites, such as "Peter Rabbit" and "Red Riding Hood." The children are taught to use book-markers of paper to indicate the pages which they wish to show to others in the groups.

The second part of the story hour is a group period in which individual pupils show the class the pictures they want to share. Sometimes a child asks the teacher to read to the class the legend under the picture. As reading ability comes, through varied learnings which are taking place in class activities, the teacher finds children who can read the legends to the class.[2]

A similar picture is presented by Grace E. Storm and Nila B. Smith:

After the period when the children look at the books, there should be a period during which they may show the pictures from any book they have selected from

---

[1] Anderson, Charles J., and Davidson, Isobel, *Reading Objectives*, p. 173. Laurel Book Company, 1925.

[2] Mossman, Lois Coffey, *Principles of Teaching and Learning in the Elementary School*, pp. 209–10. Houghton Mifflin Company, 1929.

the library table. In the beginning they are satisfied to show the pictures, but soon there is a desire to read the legends under the pictures.[3]

In *The First Grade Teachers' Manual for the Child Story Readers* the relation between reading and sharing is expressed in this sentence:

Each day a definite period should be set aside at which time every child should have an opportunity to listen to and later read for himself the best books from every field of human endeavor.[4]

These references indicate that there is a need for a very young child to share his experience soon after he has read. The fact that many of these professional publications do not advocate a close relation between the library reading period and the story hour in the second and third grades indicates a belief that these children are able to retain their reading experiences better than first grade children, thereby allowing for a longer lapse of time between the library reading period and the story hour.

WORK OF THE TEACHER AND CHILDREN DURING THE STORY HOUR

While the work of the teacher and the children during the story hour is treated by a majority of the teachers and less than a third of the professional publications, courses of study lag with only one school manual reporting.

The data in Table IX indicate that the teacher should be a participating member who directs the leadership and who encourages and aids children in the sharing of their stories. Doubtless those making recommendations on this point would have the teacher truly enjoy the contributions and sense the value of bringing in new and interesting materials when it is most propitious. One can readily conceive of groups being introduced to new fields by the teacher's contributions during the story hour. Of course, such instruction presupposes a broad knowledge of children's literature.

When the activities listed in Tables IX and X are compared in the light of classroom practice, the differences found are not

[3]Storm, Grace E., and Smith, Nila B., *Reading Activities in the Primary Grades*, p. 256. Ginn & Company, 1931.

[4]Johnson, Eleanor J., *The First Grade Reading Manual for the Child Study Readers*, p. 39. Lyons and Carnahan, 1927.

TABLE IX

PERCENTAGES OF 1 COURSE OF STUDY, 7 PROFESSIONAL PUBLICATIONS, AND
165 TEACHERS REPORTING CONCERNING THE WORK OF THE
TEACHER DURING THE STORY HOUR

Work of Teacher	Percentages		
	Courses of Study	Professional Publications	Teachers
Read and discuss stories with the group.....	100.0	42.9	86.7
Call upon children to report their reading experiences............................		42.9	22.4
Aid children in making selections and preparing the reports.....................	100.0	28.6	
See that there is a wise distribution of leadership at the story hour..................	100.0	14.3	
Invite two or three children a day to read...		14.3	
Work with children in developing standards for reporting...........................		14.3	
Preside at the story hour................			40.0

significant since it is commonly conceded that teachers are supposed to teach children those things they should know. But when viewed from the standpoint of the educational philosophy expressed by these writers, this difference is meaningful. For them, the story hour is a veritable group enterprise. The teacher, as was seen above, is described as a participating member of the group who reads and discusses stories, as one who works with the children in choosing standards for reporting, and as one who en-

TABLE X

PERCENTAGES OF 1 COURSE OF STUDY, 5 PROFESSIONAL WRITINGS, AND 165
TEACHERS REPORTING CONCERNING THE WORK OF THE
CHILDREN DURING THE STORY HOUR

Work of Children	Percentages		
	Courses of Study	Professional Publications	Teachers
Organize the information and report it voluntarily............................		20.0	96.9
Organize a reading club (selecting officers) in second and third grade..............		20.0	33.3
Request the story to be heard and form an attentive audience.....................	100.0	20.0	
Formulate standards for reporting..........		40.0	57.0
Secure selections for the teacher to read.....		20.0	

courages all members to report. The group becomes lifelike by organizing a reading club and selecting a president. It assumes responsibilities among which are devising interesting methods of reporting, sharing reading experiences voluntarily, and forming an attentive audience.

CHECKING UPON THE BOOKS READ

Considerable attention is given by the three sources of information to the problem of checking upon the books read after a library reading period and a story hour have been inaugurated.

TABLE XI

PERCENTAGES OF 13 COURSES OF STUDY, 6 PROFESSIONAL PUBLICATIONS, AND 237 TEACHERS REPORTING CONCERNING THE CHECKING OF LIBRARY READINGS

NATURE OF REPORTS	PERCENTAGES		
	Courses of Study	Professional Publications	Teachers
Reports voluntary......................	38.4	30.8	69.2
Reports required.......................	46.1	15.4	24.2
Reports required of poorer readers.........	7.7	15.4	4.5
Reports required on a few of the books.....	7.7	15.4	1.2
Reports required on the most important books		15.4	

The data in Table XI show that approximately a third of the courses of study and professional publications, and two thirds of the teachers indicate that the reports should be given voluntarily. One argument in support of this position is that if the reports are given voluntarily the teacher will be acquainted with the reading done by the pupils and therefore there is no need for the checking period. Another is that voluntary reports are in keeping with the spirit of enjoyment which should prevail during the story hour. The following statement is characteristic of the opinions of several writers:

> The only form of comprehension check which may be used safely with recreatory reading is that of letting children share their enjoyment with others by telling a part of the story they like best or some voluntary form which the child is eager to make after reading the selection. . . .[5]

[5]Storm, Grace E., and Smith, Nila B., *Reading Activities in the Primary Grades*, p. 42. Ginn & Company, 1931.

However, the highest percentage of the courses of study do not subscribe to the above argument. Instead they recommend that reports be exacted from children. The writers of these school manuals as well as those of a few professional publications and teachers who take a similar position are doubtless skeptical of the story hour as a means of checking upon the reading done, and they fear that bad habits will result if checking is not done.

The questionnaire shows that only 17.6 per cent of the first grade teachers require reports, as compared with 35.8 per cent of the third grade teachers who do not. The reasons for this are that the third grade child is more mature and is able to account for more of his readings. But probably more significant is the fact that in the first grade the library books play a minor part in teaching children the reading mechanics, while in the third grade more dependence is placed upon these materials for teaching the reading skills.

There is little evidence in Table XI to support the practice of requiring reports from the poorer readers or reports on only a few books.

TYPE OF REPORTS USED FOR SHARING READING EXPERIENCES

While there is no information contained in professional publications and courses of study on the type of report that is best for the sharing of reading experiences, 165 teachers indicated the types of report used in their classrooms. The highest percentage of teachers used "individual oral expression" and "dramatization." The information from teachers leads one to question the advisability of using written reports with young children. There is little evidence to support this practice in the first grade and there are very few teachers who would have second and third grade pupils write reports. The latter statement is also true with regard to "reports dictated by pupils and written by the teacher," and one wonders, when this information is considered in the light of the recent study which shows that children respond willingly when invited to tell their experiences while an adult writes them,[6] if teachers are making as profitable use of this means of reporting as they should.

---

[6]Betzner, Jean, *Content and Form of Original Compositions Dictated by Children from Five to Eight Years of Age.* Contributions to Education, No. 442. Teachers College, Columbia University, 1930.

BOOKS FOR THE LIBRARY READING PROGRAM

The need for guiding teachers in the selection of library reading materials is evidenced by the suggestions made by thirty courses of study and twenty-one professional publications. Of these, twenty-one courses of study and seven professional publications recommend lists of their own making. Many of these are not as comprehensive as they should be, and show evidences of hasty compilation. There is not a well-known reading list included among the recommendations of courses of study. Furthermore, many of the school manuals do not refer teachers to the reading lists published by their local libraries.

TABLE XII

PERCENTAGES OF 30 COURSES OF STUDY AND 21 PROFESSIONAL WRITINGS
RECOMMENDING BOOKS FOR THE LIBRARY READING PROGRAM

READING LISTS	PERCENTAGES	
	Courses of Study	Professional Publications
The Twenty-Fourth Yearbook of the National Society for the Study of Education.....................		19.5
Lists published by the American Library Association....		9.6
One Thousand Good Books for Children (Bureau of Education)		9.6
M. L. Terman and M. Lima, Children's Readings......		9.6
C. Washburne and M. Vogal, Winnetka Graded Book List...		9.6
E. D. Starbuck and F. K. Shuttleworth, A Guide to Literature for Character Training.................		4.8
Lists made by the writer of course or book...........	70.0	33.3

Included among the recommendations of the professional publications are six well-known book lists. These are very good, but many other helpful aids are not included. It would seem that teachers should be acquainted with publications on current juvenile literature. Four magazines that are useful guides are the *Horn Book*, the *Saturday Review of Literature*, the *New York Times Book Review*, and the *Herald Tribune Book Review*. Many teachers need not only lists of suggested books but instruction in selecting children literature. These teachers should be referred to such books as *Adventures in Reading* by May L. Becker, *First Experi-*

ence with Literature by Alice Dalgliesh, and *Realms of Gold in Children's Reading* by B. E. Mahoney and E. Whitney.

Table XIII shows that four of the ten kinds of books listed are recommended by each of the three sources. These are realistic stories, fables, factual material, and pictures. With the exception

TABLE XIII

PERCENTAGES OF 30 COURSES OF STUDY, 21 PROFESSIONAL PUBLICATIONS, AND 146 TEACHERS RECOMMENDING BOOKS FOR THE LIBRARY READING PROGRAM

READING MATERIALS	PERCENTAGES		
	Courses of Study	Professional Publications	Teachers
Kinds of Materials			
Fanciful stories..........................	3.3		62.3
Realistic stories.........................	3.3	23.8	35.1
Fables..................................	13.3	23.8	38.4
Factual material........................	16.6	19.6	32.9
Picture books and picture collections.....	50.0	14.3	10.3
Poetry.................................	6.6		27.5
Classic literature.......................		4.8	
Silent reading checks...................		4.8	
Puzzles................................		4.8	
Humor and wholesome nonsense.........	3.3		
Form and Quantity of Materials			
Readers...............................	13.3		52.8
Magazines and papers..................	15.5		27.5
Advertising materials..................			0.7
Materials made by the teacher and children	3.3		
One copy of a large number of books......	3.3		
Books that are in good condition.........	6.6		
Books that are made of linen or cardboard	3.3		
Range and Grade of Materials			
Wide range of interesting books..........	26.4	33.3	
Easy, medium, and hard books..........	33.3	19.5	
Familiar stories........................	3.3		
Books adapted to the individual needs....	19.8	4.8	
Materials not used in the recitation period...........................		9.6	

of poetry and fanciful stories standard book lists give very little attention to the types of reading materials not supported by each of these sources of data. In the light of the practical use made of fanciful stories and poetry, as shown by the data from teachers, it seems that the majority of the courses of study and professional publications have failed to give teachers guidance on materials which they use.   Even though the use of classic literature and materials to improve study habits is given very little support, there is no reason to believe that some of this material cannot be used advantageously in the library reading program.   Considerable use is made of fables.   This practice is seriously questioned by some students of literature.

Indications are that the typical course of study and professional publication included in this study give very little information on the materials that should be used in connection with the reading program.   And the average teacher who reported the books she was using is in greater accord with the suggestions of standard reading lists than are the recommendations of the typical course of study and the typical professional publication.

The information on the form of the library reading materials shows a use of the varied types of materials found within the environment.   There is some use of magazines, papers, advertising matter, and materials made by the teacher and the pupils.   It is recommended that only one copy of the same book be used and that the books be in good condition.

Considerable attention is given by courses of study and professional publications to generalizations on the range and the grade of materials to be used.   According to these writings there should be a variety of interesting materials that are suited to the varied reading abilities found within the classroom.   Thus in some books the text should be easy, in others it should require more effort to understand, and in still others it should be difficult.

SELECTING THE LIBRARY READING MATERIALS

Four professional publications and two courses of study of the groups examined make recommendations concerning the method of selecting books.   The suggestions made by the professional publications are that the teacher should instruct children in the evaluation of books and that books should be selected by the teacher and the children.   An exception in this case is made by one publication which advises teachers not to allow definitely worthless books to come before the children.   The two courses of study recommend that each class select a committee of three to choose books from the branch library, and that the teacher determine whether the books are suitable for the class.

SOURCE OF LIBRARY READING MATERIALS

Approximately 70 per cent of the teachers reporting in this study state that they secure books for the library reading program from the school library. Even though one is inclined to criticize some boards of education for not furnishing at least some of the books for this program, it must be remembered that the library phase of reading in the primary grades is relatively new, and some boards have not been able to meet this demand. The courses of study and professional publications giving information on the source of books do not mention boards of education. But it is believed that they assume that some of the materials should come from this source.

Table XIV shows that the most frequently suggested sources are the home, the public library, and the materials made by the teacher and the children.

TABLE XIV

PERCENTAGES OF 17 COURSES OF STUDY, 10 PROFESSIONAL PUBLICATIONS, AND 254 TEACHERS MAKING SUGGESTIONS ON THE SOURCES OF READING MATERIALS

SOURCES	PERCENTAGES		
	Courses of Study	Professional Publications	Teachers
Loan or contribution from the home.......	23.5	50.0	57.1
Loan from the public library..............	35.4	40.0	23.2
Made by the teacher and the children......	17.7	40.0	41.0
Contribution by parent-teacher association..	17.7	10.0	23.2
Contribution by the children.............	58.8	10.0	21.6
Contribution by the class................		10.0	
Contribution by the teacher..............	17.7		46.5
Exchange books with another class........	17.7		

There is no information to show how fruitful any of these sources are, but probably the public library is more so than the home, and certainly it is more so than the materials made by the teacher and the children. Only 23.2 per cent of the teachers report that they secure books from the public library. This is probably due to the fact that this specialized service for children is relatively new, and it will be some time before many public libraries will be able to meet this demand. A statement from the Report of the Reading Committee of the White House Conference on Child Health and

Protection[7] reveals that there are more children's books in the home today than ever before, but there "are still thousands of homes without books or magazines suited to children, and there are indications that home libraries play a relatively unimportant part in the reading experiences of American children."

It is reasonable to believe that a few of the books can be secured from each of the remaining sources listed in Table XIV. Even though this number be small the demands of the parent-teacher association, the children, and the teacher will make them feel a certain amount of responsibility for supplying the library reading table with books.

One reason given by teachers for making materials is the dearth of written matter for very young children. This need is being met and in all probability an ample supply of materials for the primary grades will be available within the near future.

PREPARATION OF READING MATERIALS

Because of the emphasis upon home-made or teacher-made reading materials this problem was included in the questionnaire, and answered by 114 teachers. Of the first grade teachers taking part in this study 47.4 per cent have made reading materials for their classrooms. This percentage decreases in the second and third grades to 37.8 and 35.9 respectively. This is probably due to the fact that more materials are available for the second and third grades than for the first grade. There seems to be no doubt that child experience reading which forms a larger part of the beginning reading program accounts for some of this small difference.

The motives for producing home-made materials are mentioned by all who are engaged in this work. Table XV shows that the reasons given differ but slightly according to grades, with the exception of the items "Revise reading matter that is too difficult" and "Furnish information for solving some classroom problems." The dearth of materials which first grade children are able to read makes it imperative that the teachers in this grade do much more revising than third grade teachers; thus it is not surprising that the item was checked by only 14.3 per cent of the third grade teachers and by 42.0 per cent of the first grade teachers. This, however,

---

[7]White House Conference on Child Health and Protection. "Children's Reading," p. 13. The Century Company, 1932.

does not explain the difference in number of first and third grade teachers who make materials to meet some classroom problem, for such problems arise in both grades, and pictures and illustrations are an excellent medium for clarifying ideas regardless of grade. We may assume that the class activity furnishes a strong motive for the production of home-made material in the third grade, but that first grade teachers are kept busy revising texts which might be used to solve classroom problems but are too difficult for the children.

TABLE XV

PERCENTAGES OF 50 FIRST GRADE, 29 SECOND GRADE, AND 35 THIRD GRADE
TEACHERS GIVING MOTIVES FOR PREPARING READING MATERIALS

MOTIVES	PERCENTAGES			
	Grade 1	Grade 2	Grade 3	All Grades
Revise reading matter that is too difficult for the children..........	42.0	27.9	14.3	28.1
Give the children a new story or information not otherwise available..	56.0	62.1	54.3	58.5
Aid the children in their activities...	74.0	58.6	71.4	67.6
Provide the child with a means of utilizing his leisure time..........	40.0	34.5	42.9	39.4
Furnish information for solving some classroom problem..............	22.0	34.5	40.0	32.4

This brings us to the question of the children's part in the making of these materials. According to the questionnaire, approximately 62 per cent of the teachers in each grade enlist the children's aid in making reading materials.

TEACHING CHILDREN TO USE AND CARE FOR BOOKS

Little attention is given by courses of study and professional publications to specific things that should be taught children concerning use and care of books (see Table XVI). Teachers were not asked to give information on this point. It must not be assumed that a large percentage of the writers of professional publications and courses of study do not hold it important to teach children to use the table of contents, index, marginal headings, and markers, for such has long been considered a part of basal reading instruction. But one is inclined to believe that the use of the public library, the arrangement of the books, and the checking in and out of books

TABLE XVI

PERCENTAGES OF 6 COURSES OF STUDY, AND 4 PROFESSIONAL PUBLICATIONS
MAKING SUGGESTIONS CONCERNING THE USE AND CARE OF BOOKS

| | PERCENTAGES | |
SUGGESTIONS	Courses of Study	Professional Publications
Train and assist librarians to check books in and out....	33.3	25.0
Teach children to arrange books......................		50.0
Teach children to draw books from the library.........		25.0
Teach children the responsibility for returning books on time..		25.0
Work with children in formulating rules on the care and the use of books (Keeping books clean)...............	33.3	
Teach the children how to use the table of contents, index, marginal headings, markers, and how to open new books and to turn pages..........................	33.3	50.0
Teach children to use the public library..............	50.0	

TABLE XVII

PERCENTAGES OF 10 COURSES OF STUDY, AND 9 PROFESSIONAL PUBLICATIONS
RECOMMENDING SPECIAL MEANS FOR INTERESTING CHILDREN IN READING

| | PERCENTAGES | |
MEANS OF STIMULATING INTEREST IN READING	Courses of Study	Professional Publications
Encourage children to purchase books................		11.1
Have children select books for the library reading table..		11.1
Have children earn money to purchase books..........		11.1
Have children assist in running the library............		11.1
Make trips to the library to explain to the children the collections and the system of checking books in and out	40.0	22.2
Give special programs, dramatizations, pageants.......		11.1
Use posters advertising books......................		11.1
Have children make furniture needed for the library reading program................................		11.1
Provide an abundance of interesting materials.........		11.1
Provide a motive for reading to find out how to make a sailboat, how to make a candle, etc................		11.1
Make records of children's readings..................		11.1
Give certificates or credit for reading a certain number of books...		11.1
Change books on library table frequently.............	30.0	11.1
Organize summer reading clubs......................	10.0	
Encourage children to check books for the public library	20.0	
Post a monthly list of worth-while books.............	10.0	
Post individual records............................	10.0	
Visit the story hour at the public library with the group	20.0	

can best be taught primary children in conjunction with the library reading program where there is a need for this information.

MEANS OF STIMULATING INTEREST IN READING

In addition to making provision for a story hour, a reading period, and a teacher to help children over all kinds of obstacles, there are nineteen suggestions given by ten courses of study and nine professional publications for interesting children in books. The suggestions are varied and touch many phases of the child's life in and out the classroom (Table XVII).

There is considerable diversity of opinion and no marked agreement among the courses of study and professional publications, a fact which indicates that there are many ways of stimulating children to do more reading. The use of credit and certificate as a reward for children's reading and the posting of individual records are the only activities listed that might be seriously questioned. The motives are external to the reading. Therefore any emphasis upon these activities will motivate reading, not for the satisfaction afforded but for the credit and certificate.

HOME READING

There are seven professional publications and nine courses of study that advocate home reading, and 250 teachers that use it in conjunction with the library reading program. It is readily seen that great importance is attached by teachers to this phase of the library reading program. Approximately 60 per cent of the teachers encourage the children to take their books home to read and share with others, and approximately the same percentage encourage the parents to become interested in their children's readings. Further, 40.8 per cent of the teachers would have parents aid the child in securing books. Thus the library reading program has added another task to the work of the teacher—that of educating the parents to play a part in shaping the child's reading environment.

RECORDS

Table XVIII shows that 23.1 per cent of the courses of study and 14.3 per cent of the professional publications use records as a means of stimulating interest in reading, and that 7.7 per cent of the courses of study and 14.3 per cent of the professional publications use records as a suggested reading list for other pupils. In addition, 23.1 per cent of the courses of study use records as a measure of children's readings, and 14.3 per cent of the professional publications use records as a measure of the influence of the content subjects upon library reading. The small support given these values does not allow one to come to a definite conclusion concerning their function when records are used. But one is inclined to believe that records are most potent when used as a tool for measuring growth in reading. They reveal to the children and the teacher the progress made. There must be safeguards, however, against one danger here, and that is the competitive spirit. Teachers should be careful not to emphasize the length of the reading list.

TABLE XVIII

PERCENTAGES OF 13 COURSES OF STUDY, AND 7 PROFESSIONAL PUBLICATIONS
STATING THE PURPOSES FOR KEEPING RECORDS

PURPOSES	PERCENTAGES	
	Courses of Study	Professional Publications
Serves as a means of stimulating interest in reading.....	23.1	14.3
Serves as a measure of the growth in reading..........	23.1	
Serves as a suggested list for other pupils.............	7.7	14.3
Serves as a measure of the influence of the content subjects upon the library reading......................		14.3

From the small amount of data available it is almost impossible to detect trends of practice in the keeping of records. Table XIX shows, however, that a higher percentage of publications recommend use of records with older children, there being only one professional publication that advocates records in the first grade and only four courses of study suggesting that they be used in the first and second grades.

Concerning the person who shall keep the record there is almost equal evidence to support the practice of the teacher's keeping the record or the child's keeping the record. This division of opinion would indicate that there are other factors that determine the choice of a recorder. Probably the child's ability in writing would determine in part whether he or the teacher should keep the record.

TABLE XIX

PERCENTAGES OF 13 COURSES OF STUDY, AND 7 PROFESSIONAL PUBLICATIONS
GIVING INFORMATION ON THE KEEPER OF THE RECORDS

KEEPER	PERCENTAGES	
	Courses of Study	Professional Publications
Children in the first grade............................	7.7	
Teacher in the first grade............................	15.4	14.3
Children in the second grade.........................	7.7	14.3
Teacher in the second grade.........................	15.4	28.6
Children in the third grade..........................	7.7	42.9
Teacher in the third grade...........................	38.4	14.3

THE TIME OF YEAR FOR BEGINNING THE LIBRARY READING PROGRAM IN THE FIRST GRADE

All the professional publications, courses of study, and reports from first grade teachers used in this study advocate the use of library materials in the first grade, but they do not recommend that this reading matter become an important part of the reading program before the child is an independent reader.   There are 74.4 per cent of the seventy-eight first grade teachers, 50.0 per cent of the six courses of study, and 71.5 per cent of seven professional publications that advocate the use of library reading materials before the children learn to read.   The position taken here is that the use of the library table with its attractive books is one means of creating reading readiness.   This view is clearly expressed in Marjorie Hardy's *Second and Third Grade Manual:*

Before a child can be expected to have a desire to explore unknown material (books), he must have an opportunity to become interested in material other than his own chart material (known material).   Therefore, it is important that the beginner be introduced to the books the first day of school and every day thereafter. This means that the teacher should encourage children to bring books to school to show to the group and to be left on the schoolroom table for children to look at.[8]

A different view is expressed by 21.8 per cent of the seventy-eight first grade teachers, 28.6 per cent of the seven professional publications, and 50.0 per cent of the six courses of study.   For them the library reading program should be used after the children have gained some knowledge of reading.   They express the fear

[8]Hardy, Marjorie, *Second and Third Grade Manual*, p. 149.   Wheeler Publishing Company, 1926.

that children will drift into bad reading habits if allowed to browse into a variety of reading materials when first introduced into reading. A statement from W. S. Gray shows that while he would use library books with young children when proper conditions are provided, he recognizes the dangers involved in this use of these books. He says:

Many teachers are encouraging pupils to read independently before sufficient progress in reading has been made, or provide materials that are more difficult than first grade pupils can reasonably expect to read. As a result, many pupils acquire careless, indifferent habits of reading or actually cultivate a distaste for it. The point which merits vigorous emphasis at this point is that the early ages of free reading require a careful direction, guidance and study by the teacher as does pupil participation in other types of reading activities.[9]

THE FURNISHINGS NEEDED FOR THE LIBRARY READING PROGRAM

The need for a table in the primary classroom for the library reading program is indicated in Table XX. While most of the data from the three sources of information support the use of a table, they reveal that there is a substantial minority that use shelves. Many of the teachers, courses of study, and professional publications recommend that the shelves be used in conjunction with the library reading table.

TABLE XX

PERCENTAGES OF 19 COURSES OF STUDY, 23 PROFESSIONAL WRITINGS, AND 230 TEACHERS MAKING RECOMMENDATIONS ON THE FURNISHINGS NEEDED FOR THE LIBRARY READING PROGRAM

FURNISHINGS	PERCENTAGES		
	Courses of Study	Professional Publications	Teachers
Tables..................................	68.4	78.2	77.9
Shelves.................................	26.4	21.7	45.8
Bookcase................................			07.4
Chairs..................................		08.7	
Tablecloth..............................	05.3		
Flowers and plants......................	10.6	04.4	
Pictures for the wall...................	05.3		
A library corner........................		13.1	
Rug.....................................	05.3		

⁹*A Better Beginning in Reading for Young Children and Modern Trends in Teacher Preparation and Teacher Guidance*, p. 15. Bulletin of Childhood Education, Washington, D. C., 1932.

It is surprising that so little information is given on the seating arrangement around the table when many professional writings and courses of study advise that the children be allowed and encouraged to browse frequently at the library reading table.

The furniture used reveals to some degree the comparative freedom upon which the library reading is based. Books are not kept in a closed bookcase but are placed on open shelves or on a table which occupies the most inviting corner of the classroom. The questionnaire yielded some interesting statements:

> We used orange crates to make shelves.
> We used both (table and shelves) when not crowded.
> We use a shelf for hard books and a table for easy books.

Such statements show that the furniture used is not of a definite type prescribed by some course of study and ordered by the supervisor or superintendent, but is made or required as the children and the teacher realize the need for such equipment. The library corner is made to look attractive because the group has decided that it should be that way. The little chairs around the table are given a new coat of paint because the group desires their furniture to look fresh. They make their own rules; the hard books are placed on one table and the easy books on another. Such things are the result of a philosophy of freedom, of choice, and of enjoyment.

CHAPTER IV

RECOMMENDATIONS AND CONCLUSIONS

THIS study has been undertaken to examine (1) the objectives for library reading and their origin, and (2) the techniques used for conducting the library reading program. The data reveal the following facts.

FUNCTION

1. That the library reading program is used as a means of realizing the two objectives: "Develop strong motives for and permanent interest in reading" and "Develop rich and varied experience through reading." The wide use of these two objectives among the advocates of library reading in the primary grades is evidence of the value of this program in developing permanent interest through the use of varied reading matter.

These objectives came as a result of a recognition of the child's reading interest and the reading proclivities of certain sections of adult life.

TIME DEVOTED TO THE LIBRARY READING PROGRAM

2. That supervised periods should be provided for the reading of library books and for the sharing of these experiences. The child should be given the privilege of using these books at his leisure. There is evidence that the reading and the sharing should occur in the first grade during one period, but as the children become more mature two periods should be provided, one for the reading and one for the sharing of experiences. Correspondingly, there is a gradual decrease in the frequency of the library reading period and a story hour from a daily occurrence in the first grade to approximately once a week in the third grade. This is probably due to the fact that children in the third grade do more leisure reading, and share only a very small portion of what they read.

The practicability and the desirability of these trends are evident when it is considered necessary for teachers to guide young children in the use of library materials, and when the story hour is viewed in the light of certain claims, which are: it stimulates interest in reading, provides a means for checking reading experiences, furnishes an opportunity for oral expression, develops discriminating tastes, furnishes an opportunity for introducing new books, and aids in class coöperation.

WORK OF THE TEACHER

3. That the work of the teacher during the library reading period should be that of removing all handicaps which might impair the enjoyment of reading, giving special assistance to slow and weak pupils, making note of the bad reading habits for correction during another period, aiding children in preparing stories to share, stimulating interest in reading materials, working with small groups, and sharing reading experiences with individuals and small groups.

During the story hour the teacher should become a participating member of the group, directing the leadership and aiding the children in the sharing of their stories.

It is evident that the value of these periods may be determined to a great degree by the teacher and her objectives. Certainly it must be said that the duties delegated to the teacher are in keeping with the objectives which would have the library reading program develop permanent interest in reading through a rich and varied reading experience.

WORK OF THE CHILDREN

4. That some of the responsibility for conducting the library reading program should be placed upon the children. They should have a part in furnishing the books and in caring for them. They should feel accountable for conducting the library reading period and the story hour.

Before a teacher can hope for her pupils to accept this responsibility it is fairly evident that she must declare herself in favor of an enjoyable library reading program, and that the children must come to feel that they are partners in this enterprise. Such an approach to the reading program with the young child is certainly desirable.

MATERIALS

There is very little information in this study concerning the materials that should be used for the library reading program. It is believed that the following reading lists should prove helpful to teachers: *Realms of Gold in Children's Reading*, by B. E. Mahoney and E. Whitney; *Children's Catalog*, M. E. Sears, Compiler; *Children's Readings*, by L. M. Terman, and M. Lima; *A Guide to Literature for Character Training*, by E. D. Starbuck and F. K. Shuttleworth; *Winnetka Graded Book List*, by C. Washburne and M. Vogal; the reading lists of the American Library Association.

These materials seem suited to young children: fanciful stories, realistic stories, factual information, poetry, pictures, picture books.

These magazines should be helpful in giving information on current literature: *Horn Book, Saturday Review of Literature, New York Times Book Review, New York Herald Tribune Book Review*.

The following sources for obtaining books, which are supported by a considerable amount of data in this study, seem worthy of consideration: the home, the public library, the parent-teacher association, the children, the teacher, and materials made by the teacher and the children. These are, however, external to the school and should not be expected to furnish a large portion of the materials for an activity that has become an integral part of the school program. This is a responsibility for boards of education. The coöperation of parent-teacher associations, home, and children should be solicited as much for creating interest in the reading programs as for supplying materials.

EQUIPMENT

5. That the table is necessary equipment for the library reading program in the primary grades. The value of this piece of furniture may be determined by the ease with which children gather around it to read and make selections, and the excellent display it makes for books. Shelves may be used advantageously in con-

junction with the library table. It is also believed that the table should be kept in some quiet spot in the room, and with its immediate surroundings should be made as attractive as possible.

Further, there is evidence that this furniture is not standard equipment which is used at the behest of some external force. Rather the need for it has been felt by the teacher and the pupils before it was brought into the classroom. In some instances it has been constructed by the children. The value of having them do this work may be questioned, but certainly this method is to be chosen in preference to doing without that which is needed or providing furniture that cannot be adequately used. There are, however, no valid reasons why school systems should not attempt to furnish suitable equipment for this reading program.

TECHNIQUES

6. That the following practices are observed in conducting the library reading program:

Reports should be given voluntarily. There is some evidence that it is good practice to check upon the poor readers, but more study is needed on this point. The means employed for reporting should be "oral expression" and "dramatizations." Very little attention is directed to "written reports," but there are no reasons to believe that they cannot be used profitably with some children, especially since a recent study has shown that children give their experiences willingly to adults who wish to write them.

Children should be taught to use the books properly and to care for them. The library materials should be evaluated not by the teacher alone but by the teacher working in conjunction with the pupils.

Teachers can profitably use the following methods for stimulating interest in reading:

Encourage children to purchase books.
Have children select books for the library reading table.
Have children earn money to purchase books.
Have children assist in running the library.
Make trips to the public library to explain to the children the collections and the system of checking in and out books.
Organize book exhibits.
Give special book programs—dramatizations.
Use posters advertising books.

Have children make furniture needed for the library reading program.

Provide an abundance of interesting materials.

Provide a motive for reading to find out how to make a sailboat, how to make a candle, etc.

Make records of children's readings.

Change books on the library table frequently.

Organize summer reading clubs.

Encourage children to check books from the public library.

Post a monthly list of worthwhile books.

Visit the story hour at the public library with the group.[1]

Children are encouraged to read library books outside the classroom. This method is in accord with the broad reading objectives for library reading.

The data in this study are not sufficient to make definite recommendations concerning the value of records of each individual's readings. Neither is there sufficient evidence to make recommendations as to the person who should record the readings, but it is felt that wherever possible children should be encouraged to record the names of the books they have read.

The library reading program should be started at the beginning of the school year in the first grade. There is also evidence that this use of the library reading materials creates reading readiness. The position taken by the minority in this study, however, must not be ignored for they contend that children will develop bad reading habits if the reading program is not well planned and if the children are not given adequate supervision.

CONCLUSIONS

It is evident that the library reading program is in accord with the educational philosophy which would have instruction conform to the nature of the child. The several trends show the need for a program that allows the child freedom to make selections according to his interests, to read at his own volition, and to share the responsibility for conducting the whole program with the teacher. Further, they show the need for a great variety of interesting materials, and for a teacher who is able to guide children in their readings. Thus it seems safe to predict that future endeavors to develop a more natural approach to reading will follow these trends to a great degree.

[1] Additional techniques will be found in "Methods Employed to Stimulate Interest in Reading," by W. F. Roche, *School Review*, Vol. 37, pp. 36–37, February, 1922.

BIBLIOGRAPHY

PROFESSIONAL PUBLICATIONS

ANDERSON, C. J. AND DAVIDSON, ISOBEL. *Reading Objectives.* Laurel Book Company, 1925.

BROOKS, F. D. *The Applied Psychology of Reading.* D. Appleton & Company, 1926.

COLEMAN, BESSIE, UHL, W. L., AND HOSIC, J. F. *The Teachers' Manual for the "First Grade Reader of The Pathway to Reading."* Silver, Burdett & Company, 1925.

DAVIDSON, ISOBEL AND ANDERSON, C. J. *Teachers' Manual for the "Lincoln Readers."* Scott, Foresman & Company, 1926.

DOLCH, E. W. *The Psychology and Teaching of Reading.* Ginn & Company, 1931.

GATES, A. I. AND HUBER, M. B. *Teachers' Manual for the "Work Play Book."* The Macmillan Company, 1930.

GECKS, MATHILDE C., WITHERS, JOHN W., AND SKINNER, CHARLES E. *Manual for the "Story and Study Readers."* Johnson Publishing Company.

GIST, A. S. AND KING, W. A. *The Teaching and Supervision of Reading.* Charles Scribner's Sons, 1927.

GRAY, WILLIAM S. "Current Practices in Teaching of Reading as They Affect the Development of Desirable Types of Reading Achievement." In *Bulletin of the Association for Childhood Education: A Better Beginning in Reading for Young Children and Modern Trends in Teacher Preparation and Teacher Guidance.* (Edited by Alice Temple).

GRAY, W. S. "Permanent Interest in Reading." *Journal of the National Education Association,* Vol. 20, No. 4, p. 137, April, 1931.

GRAY, W. S. AND LEIK, EDNA B. *Teachers' Guidebook for the "Elson Basic Readers," Book Three.* Scott, Foresman and Company, 1931.

GRAY, W. S. AND ZIRBES, L. "Primary Reading." Vol. Two of *The Classroom Teacher.* The Classroom Teacher, Inc., 1927.

HARDY, MARJORIE. *The First Grade Manual for the "Child's Own Way Series."* Wheeler Publishing Company, 1926.

JOHNSON, E. M. *Manuals for the "Child Story Readers."* Lyons & Carnahan, 1928.

LYMAN, R. L. *The Enrichment of the English Curriculum.* University of Chicago Press, 1932.

McLOUGHLIN, EDITH M. *Teachers' Manual for Book One, "The American Cardinal Readers," Part II.* Benziger Brothers, 1929.

MOORE, ANNIE E. *The Primary School.* Houghton Mifflin Company, 1925.

MOSSMAN, L. C. *Teaching and Learning in the Elementary School.* Houghton Mifflin Company, 1929.

NEAL, ELMA A. *Teachers' Manual for the Second of the "Happy Childhood Readers."* F. A. Owens Company, 1930.

PENNELL, MARY E. AND CUSACK, ALICE M. *How to Teach Reading.* Ginn & Company, 1924.

PENNELL, MARY E. AND CUSACK, ALICE M. *Teachers' Manual to Accompany "Children's Own Readers."* Ginn & Company, 1929.

STORM, GRACE E. AND SMITH, NILA B. *Reading Activities in the Primary Grades.* Ginn & Company, 1930.

SUZZALLO, H., FREELAND, G. E., McLOUGHLIN, K. L., AND SKINNER, A. M. *Teachers' Manual for the "Fact Story Readers."* American Book Company, 1930.

Twenty-Fourth Yearbook of the National Society for the Study of Education. Part I, "Reading." Public School Publishing Company, 1925.

WHITE, MARGARET L. AND HANTHORN, ALICE. *Teachers' Manual for the Primer and First Reader of the "Do and Learn Readers."* American Book Company, 1930.

COURSES OF STUDY

BALTIMORE CITY DEPARTMENT OF EDUCATION. *Reading, Composition, Literature, Spelling, Handwriting Course of Study for the Kindergarten and Grades I, II, and III.* Baltimore, Md., 1927.

BALTIMORE CITY DEPARTMENT OF EDUCATION. *Supplement Number One to "The Course of Study for the Kindergarten and Grades One, Two and Three."* Baltimore, Md., 1925.

BUFFALO BOARD OF EDUCATION. *Course of Study—Reading—Grades One to Four.* Buffalo, N. Y., 1926.

CALHOUN COUNTY, ALABAMA. *A Tentative Course of Study in Reading. For the First Grade.* 1929–30.

CALIFORNIA CURRICULUM COMMISSION. *Teachers' Guide to Child Development for Kindergarten and Primary Teachers.* California State Department of Education. Sacramento, Calif., 1930.

CALIFORNIA DISTRICT NUMBER ONE. *Reading Course of Study for the First, Second and Third Grades.* Pueblo, Calif., 1928.

CHEYENNE PUBLIC SCHOOLS. *Reading Course of Study.* Cheyenne, Wyo., 1926.

COLUMBUS PUBLIC SCHOOLS. *Supplement to Primary Reading Course.* Columbus, Ohio, 1926.

CONNECTICUT STATE BOARD OF EDUCATION. *A Monograph on the Teaching of Reading.* Hartford, Conn., 1925.

CONNECTICUT STATE BOARD OF EDUCATION. *Course of Study in Reading and Literature, Second Edition.* Hartford, Conn., 1925.

DALLAS PUBLIC SCHOOLS. *Reading—Kindergarten, First, Second and Third Grades.* Dallas, Tex., 1928.

DENVER PUBLIC SCHOOLS. *Library Instruction. Course of Study.* Monograph No. 27. Denver, Colo., 1929.

DES MOINES BOARD OF EDUCATION. *Course of Study in Reading and Literature.* Des Moines, Iowa, 1924.

FORT WAYNE PUBLIC SCHOOLS. *Reading—Primary Department.* Fort Wayne, Ind., 1924.

FRESNO PUBLIC SCHOOLS. *Course of Study in Reading for Grades One to Six.* Fresno, Calif., 1927.

GEORGIA STATE DEPARTMENT OF EDUCATION. *State Course of Study.* Atlanta, Ga., 1930.

GRAND RAPIDS PUBLIC SCHOOLS. *Course of Study for the Kindergarten and First Grade.* Grand Rapids, Mich., 1927.

GUNNISON BOARD OF EDUCATION. *Reading—Grades 1-8.* Gunnison, Colo., 1925.

ILLINOIS WESTERN STATE TEACHERS COLLEGE QUARTERLY. *Reading in the First Six Grades.* Macomb, Ill., 1925.

INDIANA STATE DEPARTMENT OF PUBLIC INSTRUCTION. *Tentative Course of Study in Reading for the Indiana Public Schools Kindergarten and Grades One to Six.* Bulletin No. 107A-4. Indianapolis, Ind., 1930.

INDIANA STATE DEPARTMENT OF PUBLIC INSTRUCTION. *Manual with Course of Study for the Elementary Schools of Indiana.* Bulletin No. 47B. Indianapolis, Ind., 1924.

JOLIET PUBLIC SCHOOLS. *Course of Study in Reading, Grades 1-6.* Joliet, Ill., 1925.

LEONIA PUBLIC SCHOOLS. *Reading Course of Study.* Leonia, N. J. (no date).

LOGANSPORT CITY SCHOOLS. *Outline Course of Study in Reading, Grades 1-4.* Logansport, Ind., 1928.

LONG BEACH CITY SCHOOLS. *Reading and Literature Courses of Study for Kindergarten and Grades One, Two and Three.* Long Beach, Calif., 1930.

LOS ANGELES PUBLIC SCHOOLS. *Goals of Accomplishment in Reading for First and Second Grades.* Los Angeles, Calif., 1926.

MADISON PUBLIC SCHOOLS. *Courses of Study in Reading.* Madison, Wis., 1929.

MANITOWIC PUBLIC SCHOOLS. *Guidance in Reading.* Manitowic, Wis., 1930.

MASON CITY SCHOOLS. *Reading and Literature.* Mason City, Iowa, 1927.

MICHIGAN WESTERN STATE NORMAL SCHOOL. *Course of Study in Reading and Literature.* Kalamazoo, Mich., 1925.

MITCHELL PUBLIC SCHOOLS. *Course of Study in Reading.* Mitchell, S. D., 1927.

MUNCIE CITY SCHOOLS. *Reading.* Muncie, Ind. (no date).

NEW ORLEANS PUBLIC SCHOOLS. *Course of Study.* New Orleans, La., 1927.

PORT ARTHUR PUBLIC SCHOOLS. *Oral and Silent Reading—A Tentative Course of Study.* Port Arthur, Tex., 1928.

RALEIGH PUBLIC SCHOOLS. *Study in Reading—First Yearbook of the Raleigh Elementary Education Council.* Raleigh, N. C., 1930.

SAGINAW BOARD OF EDUCATION. *Reading in the Public Schools of Saginaw.* Saginaw, Mich., 1930.

SAINT CLOUD BOARD OF EDUCATION. *Reading in the Saint Cloud Public Schools,* by R. E. Hilpert. Saint Cloud, Minn., 1924.

SAN ANTONIO BOARD OF EDUCATION. *Course of Study in Reading.* San Antonio, Tex., 1926.

SAN DIEGO SCHOOLS. *Course of Study in Reading.* San Diego, Calif., 1928.

SAN JOSE SCHOOL DEPARTMENT. *Reading Course of Study.* San Jose, Calif., 1928.

SAN LUIS OBISPO PUBLIC SCHOOLS. *Elementary School Reading Course.* San Luis Obispo, Calif., 1930.

SHOREWOOD PUBLIC SCHOOLS. *Course of Study in Reading for the Elementary Schools of Shorewood.* Shorewood, Wis., 1930.

SPOKANE PUBLIC SCHOOLS. *Reading. Bulletin One.* Spokane, Wash., 1924.

SPRINGFIELD PUBLIC SCHOOLS.   *English—A Tentative Course of Study for Reading —Grades I and II.*   Springfield, Mass., 1929.

SPRINGFIELD PUBLIC SCHOOLS.   *English—A Tentative Course of Study for Reading, III.*   Springfield, Mass., 1930.

TRENTON PUBLIC SCHOOLS.   *Elementary Course of Study—Reading and Literature.*   Trenton, N. J., 1924.

APPENDIX

THE QUESTIONNAIRE USED BY THIS STUDY

Name................................. Grade........................

City.....................State....... School.......................

Please answer these questions. After many of them you will find possible answers, one or more of which may be your answer; if so, please place a check (√) at the left of each correct answer. If the correct answer is not given, write it in the blank space provided.

   I. Do you have library reading in your room? ......
      (Any unassigned reading is considered as library reading)

  II. What is your purpose in having library reading? Check answers.
      1. To furnish more reading material for the children.
      2. To furnish a means of using leisure time.
      3. To aid in the room activity.
      4. To enlarge the child's vocabulary.
      5. To furnish means of enjoyment that the children can share with each other.
      6. To furnish a means of stimulating permanent interest in reading.
      7. To aid the teacher in checking upon the amount of outside reading done.
      8. To furnish drill upon reading habits and skills.
      9. To give the child rich and varied experience through reading.
      10. To develop care and skill in the use of books and libraries.

III. How do you conduct the library reading in your room?
      1. When are the books accessible to the children? Check answers:
          a. At all times throughout the day.
          b. When assigned work has been completed by individuals.
          c. When assigned work has been completed by the class.
          d. During a certain period every day.
          e. During one period a week.
          f. During two periods a week.
      2. Do you have a special period for library reading? ......
          a. How often do you have this period?........................
          ....
          ....
      3. If there is a special period what do *you* do while the children are reading? Check answers:
          a. Do remedial work.
          b. Sit at the teacher's desk.
          c. Aid children who ask for help.

      d. Leave the room.

      e. Read a book.

      f. Teach another class.

      g. Correct children's posture.

      h. Correct children's manner of holding a book.

      i. Go among the children and call attention to their defects in reading; e.g., lip movement, finger pointing, etc.

4. Do you have a library table or do you have a shelf in your room?
. . . .

5. At what time of the school year do you place books upon this table or shelf?. . . . .

6. Are required assignments made from books upon the library table?
. . . .

7. Are children required to report upon books read or is it optional?
. . . .

8. When are the reports given?   Check answers:

    a. During the library reading period.

    b. During a special period called the story hour.

       1) How often do you have this period?. . . . .
. . . .

       2) What is the purpose of this period?   Check answers:

         a) To provide a period for the sharing of experiences.

         b) To provide a means of checking upon the books read.

         c) To furnish an audience situation for oral reading.

         d) To furnish an opportunity for checking grammatical errors.

         e) To furnish an opportunity for introducing new books.

         f) To aid in class coöperation.

         g) To furnish an opportunity for oral expression.
. . . .
. . . .

       3) How is it conducted?   Check answers.

         a) The class president presides.

         b) The teacher picks out some member of the class to preside.

         c) The teacher presides.

         d) The children are called upon to report.

         e) The reports are given voluntarily.

         f) The children and teacher discuss the reports.

         g) The group sets up standards for the reports.
. . . .
. . . .

9. In what form are the reports given?   Check answers:

    a. Oral expression.

    b. Oral reading.

    c. Reports written by the pupils.

    d. Teacher asking the pupils questions.

    e. Dramatization.

 f. Reports dictated by pupil, written by teacher.

 g. Informal discussion.

....

....

10. What is done to encourage home reading? Check answers:

 a. Suggest books that children can buy.

 b. Teach children how to choose books from the library.

 c. Encourage the child to take his library book home when he desires.

 d. Encourage the parent to aid the child in securing books.

 e. Encourage the parent to become interested in the child's reading.

....

....

11. What type of books are placed upon the library table or shelf for the children who cannot read? Check answers:

 a. Picture books.

 b. Drawing books.

 c. Poetry books.

 d. Stories with good illustrations.

 e. Factual material; e.g., story of an engine.

 f. Home-made material.

....

....

12. How are the new books brought to the attention of the pupils? Check answers:

 a. Introduced by the teacher.

 b. Introduced by the pupils.

 c. Introduced by placing the book upon library table or shelf without comment.

13. From what source do you secure your books? Check answers:

 a. The public library.

 b. The school library or school board.

 c. Purchased by a local organization; e.g., P.T.A.

 d. Purchased by the teacher.

 e. Purchased by the children.

 f. Secured from the child's home.

....

....

14. On the back of this sheet write the names of the books and magazines that you are now using in your library reading program.

15. Have you made any reading material for your grade that has been put into somewhat permanent form?..................................

....

 a. Why was this material made? Check answers.

  1) To revise reading matter that was too difficult for the children.

  2) To give the children a new story or information that was not available from other sources.

3) To aid children in their activities.
4) To provide the child with a means of utilizing his leisure
time.
5) To furnish information for solving some classroom problem.
. . . .
. . . .

b. Did the children help construct this material?. . . . .
. . . .

c. What grades other than yours have used this material?
. . . .